the JOURNEY

The dream of a 6th grader

SERGEI IVANTCHEV, M.D.
and co-authored by
LUCIA IVANTCHEV

©2020 Sergei Ivantchev, M.D. All rights reserved

No part of this book may be reproduced, stored in a retrieval system or transmitted by any means without the written permission of the author.

ISBN: 978-1-4567-1220-4

Printed by Howard Printing, Inc.
Brattleboro, Vermont

Dedication

It's often been said that every person has at least one book inside of him. I wrote this book for my family.

To Nicole:

I was expecting a Nick, but a princess came into the world. Remember, you're my princess. I missed so much of your childhood, but I'm amazed to see how you have grown into a beautiful young lady. God has gifted you in so many ways and I see your passion for reading and fashion. Who knows? You may be a famous designer one day. Keep dreaming and reaching to new heights, and know that…I'll be praying for you each step of the way. I am so proud of the young lady you have become.

I love you very much.
Dad

To Victoria:

I remember how I was walking so proudly with you in my arms in the corridors of the maternity hospital. It was a privilege to be present at your birth. No man was allowed inside the maternity ward at that time.

Now, after all these years you have grown into a young adult who is following in my footsteps. I am so glad you have chosen to become a physician. This is a very noble calling. I know God has very exciting plans for you. With God nothing shall be impossible. Stay faithful to Him and you'll reap a great harvest for eternity.

I love you very much.
Dad

To Lucia:

You are the love of my life. Behind every great man is a special woman. You're my inspiration and motivation. Thank you for putting up with me all these years. I am so blessed to have you as my wife. Although we've had to be apart many years, your love for God and family kept us together. You've demonstrated that love is more than just looking into each other's eyes, but looking together in the same direction toward God. I praise Him for you. You've brought into the world, and given me, the most beautiful daughters who will make us grandparents one day. I am excited about what God has in store for us.

I love you very much.

Sergei

Preface

I never realized when I found out that Sergei Ivantchev was to join me in Woodstock NB Canada for his Rural Family Medicine that I would be playing a small part in the development of the ultimately qualified collaborative care team family doctor. The paperwork told me Sergei was from Moldova. I made a point of reading about Moldova as I felt quite humbled that he had picked my practice in Woodstock for his rural experience.

After Sergei arrived I found out his choice was geographical as Woodstock was the closest choice to the Hwy 95 which was the direct route to Greenfield Massachusetts and Lucia, Victoria, and Nicole, Sergei's beloved family. I found Sergei to be a very committed Christian and dedicated to family and his goal to again be able to practice Anesthesia as he had in Moldova. This book will provide the reader the details of the very inspiring saga of Sergei and family's journey that made this possible: Moldova-Moscow-Shannon-Gander-St.John's-Ottawa-Greenfield-Halifax.

I found out Springfield area was home of many Moldovan Christians as well as the original site for basketball! Along the way Sergei acquired a Physician Assistant certificate, then MD degree in Moldova, RN in Ottawa, Master Degree in Nursing from the University of Massachusetts with a certificate as a Family Nurse Practitioner. He then came to me via Dalhousie Family Medicine Residency Program. Sergei enjoyed his time in Woodstock and his relatively easy access to family in Springfield area. I very much enjoyed Sergei's time in my practice and hearing the details of his saga. Lucia Victoria, and Nicole visited with us and we very much enjoyed hearing Lucia's side of the saga. Sergei finished the Family Medicine and his CCFP then decided to complete the circle and return to anesthesia via the Family Medicine Anesthesia program at Queens University in Kingston. Sergei did locums at URVH Hospital while at Queens and since has been the fourth member of our Anesthesia team. It was one of the highlights of my teaching career when Sergei informed me that he would be settling in our community to practice Anesthesia and keep his interest in Family Medicine by working in our evening clinic in Woodstock with Dr. Bill Mutrie and myself. Sergei's coming to work in this community adds to a significant number of students and that I currently practice with the ultimate satisfaction from teaching. In this era that all the buzzword is Collaborative Team Medicine I believe Sergei stands alone in qualifications but has actually practiced the components of the model. It has been an inspiration to meet someone this dedicated to practice his choice in Medicine and who has overcome whatever obstacles that came along. I am sure you will find this book a confirmation of the strength of the human spirit.

    A.W. McLaughlin, M.D

Foreword

It wasn't hard to notice the visitor who came to church that Sunday morning over two years ago, since everyone in our rural community and church knows most everyone else. I now ashamedly admit that I was hoping someone else would ask him for lunch after service, and was relieved when another deacon and his wife invited him to their place. Little did we realize the blessing we had missed. Thankfully, he came back to church, and we were given another chance to be hospitable to Sergei. That day at our table, my husband and I listened as he relayed in his Russian accent, story, after incredulous story, of his past, and how he came to be working as an anesthesiologist at our new hospital.

And so, began a special friendship.

King Solomon writes in Prov. 29:18 that "Where there is no vision, the people perish; but he that keepeth the law, happy is he." KJV

This book is about a man to whom God gave a vision as a young boy, and his incredible journey to the fulfillment of that vision.

Filled with often humorous depictions of his early life in the Soviet Union, and his unquenchable desire to seek a better life for him and his family, Sergei weaves his story; leaving those of us with lesser courage and commitment shaking our heads in amazement.

I know that Sergei wrote this book for his family, but I also know it will be a source of inspiration and encouragement to all who read it.

It's going to be so exciting to watch the future chapters in the lives of these precious friends unfold!

Judy Albright

Prologue

I want to thank you for opening this book, by doing so I know you will be inspired by the stories you will read that are being told through the memories my father harbored for over forty years.

When I heard these stories from my family about their experience with communism such as: my mother having to donate blood while in school so she can receive time off from school to visit her family, or my father being ridiculed and mocked by his professor for believing in God - I feel like I am hearing stories about characters in a novel, or in a movie. It is unfathomable to me to think that my own parents, and millions of others, have suffered in this way. I will never begin to understand the hills they had to climb that brought them to where they are today.

In this book, you will hear the story of how a boy growing up in the Soviet Union, came to be a doctor who has now traveled back to his native country of Moldova to administer medical care to those suffering with ailments in the villages, this is my father. You will hear stories of a woman who had a family, a career in the perfume factory that fulfilled her, and no desire to leave all she knew behind. You will read about her post immigration years when she became a school district's very first Romanian and Russian tutor and Interpreter, and a cosmetologist who is impacting men and women of all ages. This woman is my mother. You will also read about a girl who was born in Moldova, grew up in Canada, became a figure skater at six years old and is now following her father's footsteps and is going to be a doctor. This is my Sister. You will encounter people throughout this book who have all played their own part in my father's journey, that became a family journey, which is still being written.

If you haven't guessed yet, my name is Nicole Ivantchev, the youngest in the family. I welcome you to sit back, have your tea or a snack near, and start your own journey through this book that will either leave you motivated and ready to start your own journey towards a better life, or leave you thankful for the blessings that you have and may take for granted at times.

Nicole Ivantchev

Table of Contents

Chapter 1:   The dream of a 6th grader 1
Chapter 2:   Studying well is the best defense 3
Chapter 3:   Your neck is not fat enough................................... 5
Chapter 4:   The night call... 7
Chapter 5:   Honeymoon 9
Chapter 6:   Women's Day.. 11
Chapter 7:   Welcome Victoria 13
Chapter 8:   The Coup 15
Chapter 9:   The trip to Odessa 17
Chapter 10: Invitation to Cienfuegos 19
Chapter 11: Airfare 21
Chapter 12: Good Bye 23
Chapter 13: Sheremetevo-2 25
Chapter 14: Gander, Newfoundland 29
Chapter 15: You have brought us to hell................................ 33
Chapter 16: Welcome to Regatta's apartments 37
Chapter 17: Waiting for the hearing.. 39
Chapter 18: My first car.. 43
Chapter 19: The hearing... 47
Chapter 20: What's next?.. 51
Chapter 21: Welcome to Ottawa 55

Chapter 22: Green Card 59

Chapter 23: Welcome to United States 61

Chapter 24: Moldova visit 65

Chapter 25: Me becoming an RN, and Lucia a cosmetologist 69

Chapter 26: My parents' arrival 73

Chapter 27: Welcome Nicole 75

Chapter 28: My nursing career begins 79

Chapter 29: Graduate School 83

Chapter 30: Department of State 87

Chapter 31: Residency training 91

Chapter 32: Anesthesia training 95

Epilogue: 99

Chapter 1
The dream of a 6th grader

Ivan Pavlovich left the classroom after giving us an assignment to color the atlas of Canada accordingly to each province main industry. I remember looking at the blank map and the wheat ears symbols caught my attention. These were preprinted over the center of the country and to the west, where Manitoba and Saskatchewan are.

Wow, I said to myself, this country has plenty of wheat, and probably they never had to endure lack of bread on their tables. And here my thoughts flew back in time to my grand parents' and my mother stories about not having enough bread because of forceful collectivization enforced upon people by Stalin, and their deportation to Siberia as enemy of the state. The hunger they had to endure during those years was beyond any imagination.

I wonder, how are these people in Canada doing? Is it really very cold there? Ok, I am going to color the wheat fields in yellow, just ready for harvest. Looking at the map more towards the east I saw the city of Montreal. It is in bold letters, perhaps is the biggest city over-there I thought. Man, if I can only go there for a moment to see the beauty of it. Our state run TV did not show much about western society, so I didn't have any idea what it was like. One thing I remember for sure, I loved the Canadian hockey team because often they would win over the Czechoslovakian team which beat the USSR in world cup that year. I was happy that at least there was a team who could stand tall against the Czechoslovakians.

After a few more minutes I heard the teacher's light steps in the corridor. He came back and asked us how we were doing with the geography lesson. Should I tell him that I was almost ready? How about the desire to go there and see it with my own eyes? I don't think it was a good idea because we were the pioneers, the future of youth communist party. We should not bother with the westerners, where the capitalism system is standing with one foot on the edge and with the other foot stepping in the cleft. Our bright future has been promised by our grandfather Lenin, and the communist party is guiding us surely there. We live in an advanced socialism society and by mid 80s we will reach the communism. And the years went by.

Chapter 2
Studying well is the best defense

As we were going out of the main campus, two of my class mates asked me if they can come to visit my place where I was living while at college. See, I did not live in the student dorm where most of the students lived, so they were curious to see my apartment. I was different in their view because did not go to night bars or popular disco places, tried to use clean language, did not smoke, etc.

When we got to my place, I invited them in, and while I was using the washroom, they searched my desk where I had several books and a Bible. The second day I learned that they took only a hand –written hymnbook and gave it to the history of the communist party class professor.

Without any suspicions, I sat down behind my desk while she was checking the attendance. Usually she doesn't ask me at the beginning of the class, however I was caught by surprise hearing my name called. What was the homework for today? She asked me.

The work of Lenin "What is to be done?" I replied. That is right. So, what should I do with this? And she picked and lifted up the handwritten hymnbook by one corner only, as it was infected with something in order to be seen by the whole class.

"I can't believe my eyes! She raised her voice. That is foolishness. Most of the class started to laugh. I felt embarrassed initially and did not raise my eyes from the floor. It was very humiliating experience.

You are a future professional in the medical field and you are reading this? What kind of education are you getting out of it? I felt saying back to her the words Jesus taught: "Give what is Caesar's to Caesar and what is God's to God", but didn't, knowing that will not be able to change her mind. Instead I said that I am prepared for this class and have done my homework.

For three more years I had to work extra hard in order to prove myself. Studying well was my best defense. The knowledge worked in my favor and I am so glad I used any free time to gain more and more. At the time of graduation, we had to pass four state exams. One of them was Marxism-Leninism. The same professor was one of the main examiners on this subject. Thanks God, she did not bring up my religious believes during the examination, but I could see it in her eyes trying to penetrate my mind.

At the end I succeeded. The "Red Diploma" which is similar to High Honors was given to me by the college director along with a letter of recommendation to go to medical school. The only one from the whole class of 22, the right to enter medical school without working for 2 years as a nurse or physician assistant. I was really happy for this achievement.

Chapter 3
Your neck is not fat enough

June 1989, the temperature outside + 30C and the whole graduating class of 180 is awaiting the specialty placements according to the needs of the Ministry of Health. No air conditioning in the auditorium B. We were called in alphabetical order according to our last names. When I got my turn, the dean presented me before the committee made of medical school officials, representatives from the ministry of health of the Soviet Socialistic Republic of Moldova and chaired by the minister himself.

Starting from the second year of studying I was attending the students' pediatric surgery scientific circle, and during the 4th, 5th and 6th year I have attended the all union (USSR) students' scientific conferences on pediatric surgery. In Rostov-on-Don and Dnepropetrovsk I had presentations, so the committee members were well informed.

"Well, we see you want an internship in pediatric surgery:" said the vice-minister. This year quota is only for two pediatric surgeons, he continued.

There is a need for a pediatric surgeon in Cahul, (25 miles from my hometown); however, it has been taken by one of your classmates. I knew who was that one, his father was the head of the department of urology at the Republican clinical hospital and a lecturer at the medical school. In my heart I felt saying that he will never go to Cahul because he is from Chisinau, the capital and his father will find for him a position at the republican hospital, but I didn't say anything in this regard. Who am I? Just an ordinary graduate, my father is just a carpenter, and "my neck is not fat enough".

The other position was given to the class president who was also a member of the communist party and secretary of students' communist party at the medical school.

I asked them if there is anything else close to the operating room, and they said, yes, an anesthesiology position in Tiraspol. Here, sign the acceptance letter if you want it, said the dean. "Thank you for your consideration sir:" I replied while signing it.

Well, if I didn't get the surgery, at least I can work on the other end of the OR table. This was my rationalization. In 3 weeks, I'll start the internship in anesthesia! That's not bad!

Chapter 4
The night call

A few days later I was on my regular ambulance call that I used to work part time as a physician assistant during the 6 years of medical school.

We received a call one evening at around nine, from a lady of 22 years old who was having severe foot pain and swelling, saying that she can't walk. We did not arrive until one thirty in the morning. My initial reaction was: "Why are they calling now? It is late at night! Can't she wait until morning to address her foot pain? I still have couple of weeks of classes in the morning and I would rather get some sleep. In retrospect, I could have been more sympathetic to her situation.

As these thoughts were going through my head, we arrived at destination. It is on the 8th floor said Dr. Railean, I hope the elevator works.

We entered the apartment and were talking to the patient in Russian; however, between the physician and me we discussed the case in Moldovan (Romanian language, Moldovan dialect). The lady had a case of cellulitis in her right foot that started after a cut at work. She could wait till the morning to address it; this is not a true call for an ambulance we decided. Suddenly I hear a voice behind me in Moldovan: "I understand Moldovan and don't agree with your decision!" I turned my head a saw a tall young brunette dressed in a bathrobe and with a towel wrapped around her hair. She just came out of the shower and we did not see her when we arrived. "Ok, what are you suggesting?" asked the doctor. I want you to take my friend to the hospital now. Are you going to accompany her? Yes, she said, and asked another friend to accompany her on the journey to the hospital.

The streets at night are not very well illuminated, but when we were driving next to a light pole I could see that she was beautiful, and her voice was so charming. I hoped the ride to the hospital will be longer, but we arrived in less than 10 minutes. "We are here," the ambulance driver said as he was pulling into the emergency entrance of the 4th clinical city hospital that was on call that night for all types of surgical emergencies. Here is my phone number, please call me tomorrow and update me about your friend. What is your name? Lucia, she answered. I handed her a piece of paper with the number and we left the hospital.

The second day around 5 pm I was reading something when the phone rang. I almost forgot that I was expecting a call. Hello, this is Lucia. You asked me to call you with an update about my friend. This phone call occurred in June of 1989, and we were married that August.

And the rest is history.

Chapter 5
Honeymoon

I am so glad we are going to spend honeymoon in a foreign country said Lucia. This would be our first foreign trip as a couple. Romania, just 6 month after Ceausescu's death, still had a visa regime with the USSR. The honeymoon did not happen immediately after we got married because we needed a letter of invitation from my friend in Piatra-Neamt, then obtain a foreign passport, visa and so on. Lucia did not know George and his wife Milica. I met them seven years prior when they came to Chisinau as tourists.

One night, George got sick with a high fever. They were staying at the Intourist hotel and called for an ambulance. Only foreign tourists could enter that hotel, so when we arrived there the security guy escorted us to their room. George was in bed, shivering and speaking with us in Romanian. Physician that was with me spoke only Russian, so I was the assistant and the translator. After he examined him, gave me an order to administer George an antipyretic agent with antihistamine and gave him a prescription for an antibiotic. George had a case of a strep throat. He was very happy that we understood him well and helped him. As a thank you gesture Milica gave me their address and phone number. During the next seven years, we spoke on the phone, wrote letters to each other and kept in touch, and now he sent us the invitation letter to visit Romania that was free of Ceausescu.

We took a train from Chisinau and arrived in Piatra-Neamt where

George was waiting for us with his Dacia 1300. After getting Milica we went to lacul Rosu and caile Bicazului all in the Carpati Mountains. The trip was awesome, but was just the beginning of our tour. George proposes to go to Eforie Nord, a popular tourist destination on the Black sea. They planned to take their 13-year-old daughter Laura with us as well. So, for the next 6-7 hrs the five of us were somewhat squished in his Dacia, but this did not prevent their daughter to float her ponytails back and forth in the air. That girl wouldn't sit quietly even for a minute. As she turned her head toward Milica, I felt a pinch in my right side. Lucia was trying to show me something without them noticing it. When I turned my head to the back seat I noticed several head lice crawling in Laura's hair. Large, must have been after supper. She was seating between Lucia and Milica.

The beach was great, the sand was hot, but the end of the first week we stopped enjoying it because were quite busy scratching our heads. Ironically, Lucia brought with us a few bug sprays called Dihlofos, thinking she could sell them for some Romanian money so we could have extra spending cash while on our honeymoon. She ended up selling none, as we had to use those big sprays for ourselves. Well, welcome to Romania sweetheart and happy honeymoon.

Chapter 6
Women's Day

I'll see you tomorrow morning, I told Lucia before leaving for a 24 hrs shift at the maternity hospital. By now I have completed my training in anesthesia and have been working there as an attending. It was the 7th of March, just one day before the International Women's Day. In Moldova, the 8 of March is a holiday and a very significant celebration for all. This was the time of the year when the price of flowers increased by 300%.

As for most of mothers and wives, it was a busy day for Lucia as well who also was 38+ weeks pregnant. She decided to surprise me with a gourmet dinner on this special occasion and went to the market to buy something delicious. Guess what? She wasn't alone there. Wherever store you enter, people are waiting in lines, maybe some delicate will be brought up for sale? Who knows, we just waiting in line, these were the usual replies.

During the late 80's and beginning of 90's the political and economic crisis was felt by every ordinary citizen. And the problem wasn't in the shortage of stuff, but in the artificially created deficit environment. So, people were used to have less, and appreciative when you get something been waiting for a long time.

At one of the stores she got in line to buy a fresh-cut chicken. Being pregnant one needs to go to the washroom more often. After waiting for over half hour she went to restroom, but when came back couldn't find the lady was behind her in line, so she stood approximately where she remembered her line was. This created an argument among other women there. One would say yes, I saw her standing here, the other would say no, I didn't see her here. A few minutes later one said: Hey, look, she is pregnant; we should let her go to the front of the line. Lucia had a winter coat on and her belly wasn't easily noticeable. What are you talking about? She doesn't look pregnant! Ok, ok, do you want me to unbutton my coat, here, see; now you believe?

After waiting for two hours in line, Lucia finally could purchase the chicken and other groceries so she went home to start preparing the food. In the morning on the 8th I came from work with a bouquet of pink carnations, because she really likes carnations, and I spent almost half of my night's call salary for it.

The day went smooth, we had nice dinner, went out for an ice-cream, and home to bed. In the early morning, she tells me that she was having back ache and felt the abdomen tightening up. I guess it is time, even if she wasn't 40 weeks yet. The 9 of March was my day off, so I called one of my colleague Piotr Prokopovich and asked him if he would stay home today and I'll work his shift and he can do my shift tomorrow. He agreed.

We arrived at the maternity hospital shortly before 8 am, and the chief of Obstetrics was finishing her night shift on-call. Thanks God she is still here. I asked her if she would stay and deliver Lucia, and she said yes, of course I'll if you want me to do it.

Georgeta Deomidovna was one of the most experienced obstetricians at our hospital that had over 5000 deliveries per year. She was very dedicated to her patients and Lucia felt quite relieved when I told her that she is going to be as a VIP in the hands of an excellent physician.

Chapter 7
Welcome Victoria

Delivery room was large that had seven tables and able to handle five to six deliveries simultaneously. Sorry ladies, no privacy here. We walked for a while and Georgeta Deomidovna asked Lucia to come in for an exam. You are 4 cm, and it may take some time she said. No one even asked for epidurals, as it was known to be offered only for Caesarian sections, and why does one need it? Isn't delivery supposed to be painful?

By 10:30 am the intensity of the contractions became more regular and Lucia was taken to the room. There is no such thing as husband presence during the labor. I was privileged to be there because I was the anesthesiologist on call. Fortunately, there was only one other woman in labor that delivered shortly after we enter in. You are fully dilated, let's start pushing said Georgeta. After a few pushes for some reason her contractions became weaker and just physician's words were not enough to add more strength to it. Georgeta decided to give Lucia a pill like oxytocin sublingually. Man, it was a miracle pill. After a few strong pushes a beautiful dark haired girl came into our family. It is quite a feeling; even if I was taken by surprise because I thought will be a boy. With a 3350 grams' birth weight and Apgar score 9-10, she was screaming so laud that we couldn't hear anymore the other girl born on the next table.

Congratulations, well done, shouts came from everyone around.

After I cleared my eyes and kissed her, I realized that Lucia had an episiotomy and Georgeta was going to repair it under local anesthesia. Here I can really make a difference and show off in front of Lucia, so I said that I am going to administer her some Ketamine. Georgeta Deomidovna didn't mind and Lucia had 100 mgs I/V. She didn't need any Lidocaine and liked the idea. Are you going to give the anesthetic to all postpartum episiotomies? Loudly asked Georgeta joking. Sure, I will, to all your relatives, deal?

We missed the International women's day, but gained another birthday in the family. It was the 9 of March, my father's birthday. Let's name her Victoria, in the honor of grandfather Victor, I asked Lucia. Yes, it is a pretty name, I agree, let's do it. By that afternoon I was waking carrying Victoria in my arms from the nursery to mama's 4 beds room and back. I found a "Martisor" and attached to her tiny chest, it represents a symbol of spring. She was peacefully sleeping in my arms. The words of David from the book of Psalms came to mind: "how fearfully and wonderfully we are made" …

I was thankful and happy.

Chapter 8
The Coup

Elena Ivanovna arrived very disturbed that August morning. She was the anesthetist on call and I was signing off to her after working a 24 hrs shift.

"Nam hana" she said in Russian, and told me what has been happening in Moscow the night before and in that morning. I was busy with work that didn't have time to watch the 7 o'clock morning news on TV.

Sergei Victorovich, did you see what is happening? That is, it, that's the end of Gorbachev's perestroika. "I wouldn't be surprised if I see the representatives from the military commissariat looking for us to be on alert and ready in case of any deployment" she said. In the USSR, all physicians were also getting the officer rank of military medical service, and whenever there is a need for medical personnel, they would call you up.

"Just watch, the Chisinau will be surrounded by tanks and military men, and a curfew may be declared": she continued.

I did not say much, gave her the keys for the narcotics safe and left the hospital. When I arrived home, I could see on the first channel what has been happening in Moscow, but being tired after a long shift a fell asleep. Lucia was on maternity leave and went out for a walk with Victoria in a stroller. She was only 5 months old.

Fortunately, the coup did not have a greater impact on the other republics and in Moldova the life continued as before. There was not one day without any meetings or manifestations. The Popular Front was asking for the Romanian language to be declared as a state language and reunification with Romania. The pro-Russians were demanding that the Russian language remains the state language and against unification with Romania. The main squire of the capital was blocked almost everyday by police because of these manifestations. The trolleys and buses could not circulate on their routes. At times, I was feeling that there was no control and order in the city, but chaos.

How long it will continue like that? I was getting tired of the political and artificially created economic instability. The idea of leaving the country to seek a better life and opportunities would nag me more and more.

March 1992, Moldova was accepted as a full member of the UN. This fact wasn't accepted easily in Moscow. With the presence of the 14th Russian Army in the eastern part of Moldova, mainly in Tiraspol, and support from Kremlin, an interethnic conflict started. The local self proclaimed government from the eastern part of Moldova called "Transdniester republic" hired the Kazaks form the Don region to fight against Moldovan army that was trying to have control over its territory. The Transdniestrians loyal to Russia were afraid that Moldova will join Romania and put up a fight.

From June to August as a lieutenant of medical service I was called several times in the region to help the wounded solders or perform other emergency surgeries. I could hear the Alazan type rockets flying nearby the Criuleni hospital were the surgeries were done.

The conflict ended with a cease fire in August and again I could sleep in peace at home with my wife and daughter.

Chapter 9
The trip to Odessa

I called my parents to see how they were doing, and my dad told me something I was waiting for a while to hear. He said that I should come home to talk with my friends Andrei and Katya because they are leaving soon for Canada. I remembered my dream from the 6th grade and now, after hearing that from dad, I was determined: We are leaving together. But how? What am I going to tell Lucia? She was on maternity leave and went home to her parents with Victoria. My mother in law often would say: "The air is cleaner here, and we don't have the noise you have in the city."

I took Lucia's brother's car and drove 150 km south to see my parents. I couldn't afford my own car yet, but Ivan had his car for 2 years. He worked for 8 years on a fishing ship from the port of Murmansk, and purchased his 1986 Ford Taurus in Amsterdam on his way back home. It was 9 pm when I arrived at my parents. Andrei and Katya were there waiting for me. We talked about things and later Andrei showed me a letter of invitation to visit Cuba as a tourist purchased form the Consulate of Cuba in Odessa. Moldova did not have any diplomatic relations with Cuba, and the closest mission was in Odessa, Ukraine, 180 km from Chisinau.

"You can get one as well if you want to leave with us:" said Andrei. Ok, I am leaving first thing in the morning for Odessa I said, without realizing what implications it may bring. I arrived after midnight in

Chisinau, and because I was off that day, I decided to leave for Odessa with the first diesel-train, at 6 am. At home I had multiple bottles of cognac and champagne received as gifts from the hospital, so I took 10-15 with me.

Before entering the Consulate, everyone needed to pass through an outside cabin that served as a checkpoint. The two solders were inside, a sergeant and a private. "You can't go in:" said the sergeant. O, please, I came from Moldova, and have some business to discuss inside. Here, have you tried the newest Moldovan cognac? Ok, give it to me and go. I left 2 bottles with them and when entered the reception room a blonde secretary measured me from head to toe with her strange look, and asked why I was there.

"I want to visit the island of liberty" And that it? She said laughing at me. But I didn't stop there, but continued with the fact that I am a physician from Moldova, never being to Cuba before, etc. Please, accept this gift as a friendship between the Moldovan and Ukrainian people. I could see that she wasn't Cuban, but Ukrainian that worked at the Consulate. Ok, you want the letter of invitation, isn't it? Yes, I said. She pressed a button, and I saw a man coming toward us in the corridor. I expected to see a dressed-up diplomat, but instead a 5' 6" skinny guy approached me and asked in a broken Russian. "You need a letter of invitation to visit Cuba?" You know, these letters are more expensive now. I told him that my friend Andrei got one 2 weeks ago and paid $70 for it. O no, if you want one, it would cost you $450. I did not have any choice and said Ok. "But, I am not sure if I can provide you with one at this time": he said. You can leave me you name and phone number and if I can do it, I'll call you. Thank you. Please have these Moldovan gifts, you will like it. I left the rest of the bottles, and was heading back to the checkpoint. O, our friend, good stuff. Both solders were quite happy like the sea was to their ankles only. Come again, see you later, they said as I shout the door behind me.

Chapter 10
Invitation to Cienfuegos

The next day I went to my regular shift at work, and have been praying about this letter between the cases. The later the day become, the less faith remained in me. I thought the phone will not ring that day because the Consulate was already closed.

At around 6 pm the phone rang and I could appreciate immediately by his accent that this was the man from Cuban consulate calling.

Sergei Victorovich, I have your letter, when are you coming to pick it up?

Tomorrow, I told him. "Where do I meet you?" I asked. He told me that I need to come to the Consulate at 1 pm and look for a tall, black man that will be walking there in front of the building. And don't forget the money as discussed. I understood sir, tomorrow I'll be in Odessa.

Where do I get $450 on such a short notice? I get paid in Rubles, not in dollars, and officially foreign exchange wasn't allowed without a valid travel visa to a foreign country first. I got all the dollars I had at home, and couple of thousands of Rubles. At the black market the dollar was over 100 Rubles. I counted twice, I had only $165. I am going, in faith, if he accepts the offer, I get the letter, if not, I guess, Andrei and Katya go to Cuba without me.

I arrived in Odessa on-time, came to the Consulate and was

looking around. It didn't take even 5 minutes and I saw a tall, black man dressed nice. I approached him and asked if he has a letter for me. He said; What is your name? Can I see your passport (internal passport) allowing people to travel to all the 15 republics within the Soviet Union that collapse less than a year ago? I showed him my red covered passport and he told me to walk away with him. He said that he has the letter in my name, with my wife and daughter included in it, and that he is from Cienfuegos, and inviting us to visit him in Cuba for 2 weeks.

Show me the letter, I asked him. He gave me the letter, I read it carefully, noticed that all three of us were on the invitation and that the signature of the consul and a round stamp were present. Thank you, I said, as I was returning it to him. What? Is there something wrong? You don't want it? He didn't get my move. I said, I want it, but I don't have $450 to pay for it. Ok, how much do you have? By now we got to a park and sat down on a bench. I have only $165, and some Rubles, if you accept it, I take the letter, if not, and you'll not be able to give it to someone else because it is in my name. I understand, and realize the price is high, but I don't set the prices; however, I don't have other choice, so I'll take $165. Thank you, you are truly a friend. As we talked more, he said that just a month ago he did a similar letter to someone else and the prices were $50- $70. I am sure he probably kept a small percentage for himself, and the rest the consulate workers would get. We shook hands and went our directions.

I returned to Chisinau, Lucia was still at her parents. Now, I needed to apply for a foreign passport for Lucia. I already had one as I traveled before to Warsaw and Belgrade. How am I going to get the passport without her being present? I'll get her recent black and white picture and go to the passport office. I'll find someone there who can do it. In country that is corrupt like Moldova, if you had the right connections you could accomplish getting a passport like I did for Lucia without her being present. This is one example of how eager I was to leave the country.

Chapter 11
Airfare

In three days, I had Lucia's passport for foreign travel ready. Now, the next step is to find air tickets in a short time, as the prices were changing every week. I went to the Aeroflot ticket office and found out that the price for a round trip ticket from Moscow to Havana was 70,000 Rubles, and just a week before were 50,000. I had to tell Lucia about my plans ASAP and her brother Ivan brought her and Victoria to Chisinau. After explaining to them my intentions Ivan accepted it easily because he has been overseas many times in the last 8 years, but Lucia advised me to leave alone and if I get accepted, she and Victoria will join me. Finally, we convinced her and I left to get the tickets. I had no idea that this will not be a simple process.

In Chisinau, there was only one Aeroflot ticket office for the international flights. When I got there, several people have been waiting for their tickets that were reserved a week ago. I didn't know that first we had to order the tickets, the airline "Aeroflot" which was the only airline flying to Cuba from Moscow would check the validity of visa and then one can reserve the ticket.

This must have been God's hand in it, otherwise I can't explain this. At the ticket office was a man from my hometown that drove to Chisinau to purchase his tickets for his whole family. He had 5 children, and his brother in law was leaving with him as well. They had reserved 8 tickets total for 70,000 Rubles. When my turn came to order 3 tickets to Havana the lady said that there are no tickets for the next 3-4 weeks, and that the price was already 124,000 Rubles, almost a 100% increase from one week ago.

George got his turn to the window and when the total amount was given to him, I could see his face getting pale and I thought he may pass out in shock. We sat down and it didn't take too long when he told me: "Sergei, you go" you need only 3 tickets, but I need 8. Even if I sell my car, I'll not be able to gather over a million Rubles in such a short time. When I reserved the tickets the price should have been 560,000 Rubles."

Also, the visa to Cuba would expire in a few weeks.

I counted all the money I had, and was short 60,000 because of the new prices. George lent me this amount and shortly I had the tickets in my possession. I was on my way to Cuba, but George stayed in Moldova. I believe God worked out the details and provided what I needed. There was no coincidence.

I came home with the tickets and Lucia was even more in disbelief. However, this was very real. The departure was scheduled for October 31.

Chapter 12
Good Bye

We had just enough time to drive to my parents to say good bye, and to her parents, however Lucia did not want to tell her father that she is leaving because he was sick and would not tolerate this news. Her mom escorted us to the car in tears, and we left for Chisinau. Later, her mother told Lucia's father that they had went to Romania for Sergei's medical training.

In the morning, I had to go to my hospital to give my resignation letter, but before that I went to the morning report. Usually there would be the chiefs of the departments and day shift physicians. The night shift physicians would report how the patients in ICU were; touch base regarding the scheduled surgeries for the day, etc.

At the end of the report without getting into details I told them that I was leaving to Cuba for a vacation. One of the professors said that she heard about some people going to Cuba but on their way, there they get off in Canada. In case if you want to do the same, just remember that you'll not be able to work as a physician, period. I did not say anything, but in my mind, I thought she was jealous probably, and is trying to scary me. I went to the hospital administration like human resources office and gave the letter. We did not have at that time a 2 week or 30 days' notice. The chief physician of the hospital signed the letter and the secretary made the necessary note in my work book: "Resigned for personal reasons".

In front of us was a 24 hrs train ride to Moscow and Lucia started to prepare some food for the road. I remember for sure the roasted duck along with fresh vegetables and homemade placinta were carefully placed in a plastic handbag. This was all prepared for them to have during the 24-hour train ride.

We could not take any luggage with us as it would fly to Cuba, so we took only 2 small carry on bags mostly filled with Victoria's clothes. I put on a sport costume, over it a sweater, 2 pairs of trousers, and a weekend suit on top, plus a warm jacket and a hat. I looked 50 pounds' overweight with all this clothes on me. It didn't even run through my head that the customs at the airport may be curious why I am so heavily dressed flying to Cuba. Lucia put on as many clothes she could as well and left the apartment.

Ivan drove us to the railway station. The train #148 Chisinau-Moscow was on the 1 track and we got the luggage, hugged Ivan and his friend that accompanied him and entered our car. The coupe was for 4 people, and the 4th person was a young guy that was studying in Moscow.

As the train started to move very slowly, Lucia pulled down the window to say good bye to Ivan one more time. Suddenly, she realized that she forgot the bag with the food she prepared at the apartment. She already was so stressed, and when she realized that we did not have food to eat, she cried even more. It was too late now. Ivan's friend was so happy and laughingly shouted: "Don't worry about the food; we will take care of it. I love grilled chicken"! What else he was saying we could not hear anymore… God took care of us like he always does for his children, as Matthew 6:25 says: "Therefore I tell you, do not worry about your life, what you will eat or drink; or about your body, what you will wear. Is not life more than food, and the body more than clothes? Look at the birds of the air; they do not sow or reap or store away in barns, and yet your heavenly Father feeds them. Are you not much more valuable than they? Can any one of you by worrying add a single hour to your life?" We had friends traveling on the train headed to Moscow as well who kindly shared their food with us.

Chapter 13
Sheremetevo – 2

Thirty hours later we arrived in Moscow. Even it was end of October and in Moscow is cold at that time of the year; I was so hot with all the clothes on that could not walk very far. At Kiev railway station, we walked down and took the subway train to Lucia's cousin that was studying in Moscow. The ride in the metro during a rush time hours wasn't pleasant, but got to Diana's place in 45 minutes. Victoria was tired and after some fuss fell asleep. Our flight was tomorrow afternoon.

Around noon time we left for the airport and Diana went with us to say goodbye. After an hour in metro train, we had to get on a bus running from the subway station to Sheremetevo -2. I just recall that the bus was packed to the point of not being able to breathe. Someone was pushing me on the side, and I remember saying that this is my last trip in the bus filled with hostile people and that "I am so glad I'll never have to live in this environment ever again". I must have had enough faith to say that, because at that point we didn't know whether we will be able to remain in Canada.

After arriving at the airport, we met with our friends Andrei and Katya that were flying on the same flight with us. They had their three daughters with them, the youngest being Victoria's age. No too long after the announcement in Russian came on over the speakers: Aeroflot flight SU 345 Luxembourg, Shannon, Havana ready for ticket registration and luggage check. Immediately Lucia said that they did not announce Gander. What are we going to do? The plane is not stopping in Gander for refueling?

That's not true, I thought. They just don't want to announce it, because Gander was just an intermediary airport for refueling on the flight from Shannon Ireland to Havana, Cuba.

IL 86

I knew that IL 86 can't fly more than 3500-4000 km without refueling and I said to Lucia: "We are taking this flight". If for some reason, we go straight to Cuba, we have round-trip tickets, and can come back. Fortunately, we didn't know that $54 in my packet will not last long in Cuba; otherwise this fact could have been a big stumbling block in our way.

What will we eat? Where will we stay if we land in Cuba? ...

The customs checked our luggage and the hard currency we had (dollars) and one of them started to laugh. "What are you guys going to do in Cuba with only $54" I did not have to think long and told him to read the invitation letter. It says that the person inviting us for 2 weeks to Cuba will provide everything. Ok, he said, go on to the passport control.

At the passport check point were a sergeant and a corporal. The sergeant looked at my passport and saw that it was red, the former Soviet Union style, but when he opened to the visa page for Cuba, noticed a round stamp with an eagle and asked. "What kind of stamp is that? Eagle?" I don't recognize such a stamp. I told him that I did not invented it and that was the new stamp of the ministry of external affairs of Moldova. He mourned something under his nose but I couldn't hear it.

Then he questioned us why Victoria didn't have a picture in our passports. I told him that in Moldova children up to 7 years of age are not required to have pictures when they are included in parent's passport. He got mad, and told me very officially: "Sir, you and your wife can go, but your daughter can't"! Your daughter stays!

For a moment, I was in a shock, before my eyes unveiled the useless efforts done in the last 3 weeks to get to this point., however I quickly realized that this is not so.

Please, call the officer, I asked the sergeant. Sir! (Comrade Captain), he called out.

A thin, not very tall captain came out from a cabin and looking not very happy that he was bothered, asked him: "What's wrong sergeant?" Sir, these people from Moldova don't have the picture of their daughter in the passports. Captain replied: "Where are they flying?" To Cuba Sir! "Ahhh, that means they are flying to Canada!" "F… them, let them go!" The sergeant put an exit stamp in our passports, we grabbed them and run to the boarding gate before they change their mind. Thank you, Lord, for taking us through.

Chapter 14
Gander, Newfoundland

Everyone was seated and we were flying over Europe. The next scheduled stop was supposed to be Luxembourg, however after couple of hours of flight, the captain announced that there was a thick fog in Luxembourg and we would land in Frankfurt-on-Main, Germany. We had to stay in the plane for 3 hours until the bus took the passengers to Luxembourg airport and bought back other connecting passengers flying to Shannon or Havana. Victoria was only 19 months old and although she was potty trained, because she was wearing cloth diapers and not "Pampers" because we didn't have any single use dippers in Moldova at that time and we were concerned that she might have an accident. So, we had to borrow the portable potty from another family sitting across from us who had a 12-month-old girl, and had taken their plastic potty with them on the plane. They were well prepared for a long haul.

Finally, we departed Frankfurt, and in couple of hours we arrived at Shannon airport in Ireland. There we were told that the crew would be changed, but that we wouldn't have to get out of the plane. By now it was close to midnight Moscow time and everyone was tired, especially Victoria, who fell asleep. Shortly, we saw all new stewardesses on board with fresh looking faces. "Thank God…we are continuing to fly in the same plane!" The reason I mention this, is because I found out later that in Shannon sometimes Aeroflot would change the planes from an IL 86 to an IL 62, which could fly for over 10 hours non-stop. The fact that we were still flying an IL 86 was a good sign; however, no announcements were made that our next stop would be Gander for refueling.

We were flying over the Atlantic and had been over 4 hours in the air by then, but there was still no news from the cockpit. I was sitting in a window seat and often would look out the window, but nothing… just darkness. Suddenly, I started to see lots of lights far away on the horizon. I thought "This must be Newfoundland - probably St. John's! It can't be Havana. Cuba is too far still."

After a few minutes, we heard the captain's voice in Russian first, "Ladies and gentlemen, our plane is going to land at the Gander International Airport for refueling, and then we will continue our flight to Havana".

We landed at 2 a.m. local time. The steward told us that the refueling would take around one half hour, and we had the option to wait in the plane, or go into the neutral hall inside the terminal.

Immediately, more than half of the people seated got up, took the carry-on luggage, and started to make their way to the exit door. I had to take Victoria in my arms as she was sleeping, and Lucia grabbed the 2-small carry-on bags we had, and made our way to the exit. The cold night air was felt quite well, despite the many layers of clothes we had on, as we walked over 100 meters from the plane into the airport terminal.

The plane was refueled and the announcement came on: "Flight SU 345 for Havana ready for departure."

A few Cubans and couple of Caucasian people got up and walked to the plane. The rest of us were sitting down; no one was moving. The second announcement sounded in Russian, English and Spanish, but no one moved. There were 78 people in that room. Then an immigration officer came to us and started to speak. (I thought he was yelling at us) He was pointing to the door and the plane: We thought he was probably saying something like, "Hey you, get up and go! Your plane is leaving!" But, no one was moving. We were all looking down at the floor not wanting to raise our eyes to see the officer. Another officer came, and after talking together and using a sign language, they said: "Ok, we need to collect your passports". Everyone gave them our passports. They told us to wait. It was about 3 a.m. on November 1st. During the time we waited, we could use the restroom and I remember Lucia being shocked that she could see her own reflection on the bathroom floor! Our instant impression of Newfoundland was that it had a cleanliness we never encountered before in a public area.

At 10 a.m. they started to call one family at a time. Because Andrei and Katya had three children, they went first. No one knew what was going on. Where were they taking them? Then they took the families with two children. By the time our turn came with one child, it was around 3 p.m. In front of me sat a gray-haired immigration officer, and on his desk was a speaker phone transmitting a translator's voice from St. John's.

The officer spoke in English, one sentence at a time; and then the sentence was repeated in Russian by the translator. I noticed that she was not Russian, but probably Bulgarian or Polish; but her knowledge of the Russian language was sufficient to understand what the officer was telling me: "You entered Canada illegally, without a visa, and according to the immigration law of Canada we have to deport you. Do you have anything to say in this regard?"

"Yes, I replied. I know that I entered illegally, but this was the only way to get here. We are asking for asylum. I believe that we have sufficient evidence based on political opinion and religious beliefs, to claim refugee status. I am asking you to allow us to remain in Canada until the Immigration hearing."

"Okay," he said. "Let's have some pictures and fingerprints taken."

For that moment I felt like a criminal. We were taken to a police station like I had seen only in the movies. Front profile, side profile, etc. We were so tired by now, that when I looked at the picture stapled to an 8 x 11 paper that they handed me, I questioned if this was in fact me! Hair messy, one eye larger than the other, the corner of my mouth appearing as in Bell's palsy patients. Maybe I was having a TIA, who knows?! I still laugh when I look at that piece of paper with the picture on it. This was the only official documentation we had on hand for a year and a half until the hearing. We were supposed to show it, as necessary, for identification. It scared the crap out of many reading it!

Chapter 15
You have brought us to hell

Some representatives from the Association for New Canadians came to the airport with a translator, who told us that we would be taken one family at a time to a local motel. When our turn finally came the time was 4 pm. We got into a large Chevy taxi and the driver was told by the representatives to take us to Fox Moth Motel. At that time in Gander, a semi-volunteer association had been established to help people like us who had gotten off the plane to get started with language classes and immigration paperwork.

The driver started a conversation, but I could not understand a word he was saying. I barely knew how to say "my name is," "please" and "thank you," or "I don't speak English," never mind understanding a Newfoundlander talking to me!

We could not understand why the cars driving on the opposite lane had the lights on. I realized that the evening was getting close, but outside it wasn't dark yet. Okay, I figured out…probably it is a burial cortège. We were used to see the cars driving with the headlights on during the day only if a burial was happening. I tried to ask the driver, and he probably tried his best to tell me that these cars had daytime running lights, duh!

As we drove through town, we noticed that almost every house had spider webs and lots of skeletons in front, and it felt very strange to us. Lucia was asking me: "where did you bring us, to hell"? It was a shock. I could not believe what my eyes were seeing. What kind of idol worshipers live here? I thought this was a Christian country.

Halloween decorated house

Later we found out that the day before had been Halloween. We had no idea what it was about - this was the first time we had seen it.

Finally, we arrived at the Fox Moth Motel. I went to the front desk and presented my 8x11 ID, and got the key for room 123. Victoria started to cry and be fussy, so I raised my voice so that she would stop making noise. This technique would be quite appropriate in Moldova, but it must have been strange to the lady working at the front desk, and she gave me a look that I couldn't understand. What had I done? What did she want from me?

In the room we found a new box of Kleenex and Lucia tried to open it to wipe Victoria's eyes. She turned it around, back and forth, but couldn't see how to get the tissue out, so she opened it from the side and then we went to bed early. Probably it was around 7 p.m. local time, 2 a.m. in Moscow. An hour later I heard a knock on the door. I opened and saw two young men. One was translating the other.

"We want to talk to you about Jesus Christ."

"Okay, great, come in." It did not take me long to figure out that they were not really talking to me about Jesus, but were pushing their "Book of Mormon". Respectfully, I took it and told them that I was not interested in their teaching and they left.

In the morning the cleaning lady came, and later we found the box of tissues taped with scotch tape, and opened on the top along the perforated line, and one tissue pulled out from the box as a demo for the country folks. Duh! Sorry…we didn't see this type of tissues before.

The motel had a continental breakfast and we went down to get something. In the morning Victoria liked kasha, or oatmeal with milk. We found only cereal called Corn Flakes that was different from what we were used to. "Anyway," we said, "Let's try some. But where is the milk?" Someone showed us the milk. What? Cold milk with cereals? Who eats that?!

It did not take too long for us to get acquainted with bacon, sausages and ketchup at breakfast, instead of a cup of tea or coffee with a whole wheat bagel that we were used to.

We stayed at the Fox Moth motel for a week, until the word from Immigration came that each family should decide where they want to have their hearing. Those that had some relatives or friends in Toronto, Ottawa, or Montreal were asking to be transferred there. Andrei and Katya had her sister in Toronto who had come about a month before us, and so they went to Toronto. Other families that we met at the motel went to other cities, and because we didn't have any friends elsewhere in Canada, Immigration told us that we would be going to St. John's. It was very difficult to separate from Katya and Andrei because we started our journey together. Shortly, we met another family also from Moldova who were going to St. John's as well. The representatives from the Association for new Canadians put us on a bus and told the driver that someone from the association would be meeting us in St. John's at the Water Street bus station. The 3-hour ride felt like 30 minutes because we talked all the way with this family about our new experiences in Canada.

One thing that was clear to us was that this country had organized and put into place the mechanism to meet our basic needs…and we were very thankful for it.

Chapter 16
Welcome to Regatta's apartments

By the time we arrived in St. John's was 8 p.m. and pretty dark. The streets were empty. "Where are the people?" we asked ourselves. I had a feeling that we were the only ones there.

At the bus station a lady with a Cuban translator who spoke Russian were waiting for us. We got into their dark red Chevy Astro van and drove to Dominion's supermarket.

The other family had also a daughter 2 years older than Victoria and she started to ask her parents to buy chocolate. I don't know how much money they had with them, but by now we had almost nothing in our pockets. To our surprise, the lady gave each family $130 in cash to buy groceries. She said, "This is from the Association for new Canadians and it needs to last for the whole week." We were so thankful to get cash. In Gander, they were giving us food while we were at the Motel, but no cash. Immediately I did a math calculation and told Lucia that we should have lots of money left from the groceries to purchase other necessary things. Our first purchase (and the last one for such a large amount for several years to come) was for $72. Our grocery cart was full that evening!

The van took us to the Regatta's apartments on Quidi Vidi Lake. She handed us the key for a bachelor apartment that had a crib for Victoria and a simple double mattress bed and a four-drawer dresser in the corner. The small kitchen was divided from the bedroom with a short wall that did protect Lucia and Victoria from the light when I was studying English late at night. !" Lucia liked to go for walks with Victoria around the lake. People would smile at her and say "Hello", but because she did not understand English, she was confused why they were smiling at her and what they were saying. Lucia was afraid to go back to the lake, worried someone would approach her again and she would be unable to understand them. She would watch the planes fly above her head and wish she could go back to Moldova and her family she left behind.

Nevertheless, we were grateful. I remember saying "Wow, our own apartment. We did not expect such a treat. Thank you, Lord, for working out all things together."

In the morning, we went to the Association for English classes and further instructions. I found out that I was supposed to go once a week to the Citizenship and Immigration Office to find out about our hearing date, and for them to make sure we are still there and have not caused any troubles, I guess. The bus ride was $1.00 each way and it was too expensive for me, so I walked there - around 10 km round trip. In November in St. John's it snowed and rained every day, so when I was back from one of those trips my feet were cold and wet to the bone, as my $5 boots purchased at the Salvation Army store did not perform to my expectation. "I have seen worse, so don't worry!" I would tell myself.

Welcome to St. John's. "How are you getting on, kaki? Then, with a side tilt of the head and an eye twitch,

"Yes bay!"

Chapter 17
Waiting for the hearing

Time flew by fast in the next month as we assimilated into Newfoundland's life.

At this time, because we did not own a telephone, the only way we could communicate with our family in Moldova was either through a fax machine or through letters. In the beginning of December, Lucia walked to the Association for New Canadians to check the mail. She received a fax from our friend telling her that her father had passed away. Apparently, he died just ten days after we left, but we found out this news almost two months later. When Lucia found out about her Father she began to cry and a kind worker from the Association offered to drive her home. It was the most depressing time in our family; but especially in Lucia's life. She would go down to the lake and watch the planes arriving and departing from St. John's airport every day and cry "I want to go home; I can't take it anymore" etc. Lucia had no desire to learn the language because she was sure she was going to return home. She would have liked to go to see her mom, but with no papers and no passport, if she left Canada at that stage, she would not be able to come back. It took a lot of prayers for her to accept the reality and understand the situation we were in at that point in time.

It got better when Pastor Mitchell, a missionary from Arkansas who was in St. John's working with a ship ministry in the harbor, started to visit the refugee families. He was a superman. In spite of his own circumstances, (not being young, and his wife having been killed in a moose accident a year or so before our arrival there) he was sacrificing all his time and energy on visitations. My English started to improve pretty quickly by communicating with him several times per week. In a few weeks I was asked to go with him on board a Latvian ship and a Russian ship from the port of Murmansk.

St. John's Harbor

He had hundreds of New Testaments in English and Russian and the desire was to distribute a book to each seaman. Those from Latvian ship all spoke Russian so we were able to talk to the captain and pastor Mitchell gave a short sermon for them. I translated.

I remember there were about 20 guys in that room asking different questions about God, salvation, eternal life, etc.

I was not able to get every word pastor Mitchell was speaking, but using my knowledge of scriptures, and by speaking their language, it seemed to work fine on both ships, though I was somewhat concerned that what I translated was what he did say, or explain.

That's how my involvement in the ship ministry with Pastor Mitchell started. It continued until we left St. John's one year and a half later. Some days he would take me to visit other Russian speaking families and talk to them about God. I remember many times they would not open the door, or hear from others saying; "Here comes Mitchell with his agent," as if I was from KGB or something.

By the middle of January one school bus wasn't sufficient to take all the people to church, so one Sunday the church rented 3 buses to bring the people. I counted that day; there were 130 people in that church gym listening to Pastor Mitchell. Upstairs in the sanctuary the main service was going on, and in the gym the refugee families were listening to Pastor Mitchell's sermons initially translated by another man, and after a month or two he used me to do that. It was a privilege to serve God in that capacity. However, many came for different reasons, and when they found that the church really didn't have any say or be of any help to them in getting a positive result from the immigration hearing, they stopped coming.

But for those who wanted to go to church, the 15 passenger First Baptist church van came every Sunday by the apartments to take us to church. At times it was full, at other time just my family and one or two other families would come. In July Lucia and I got baptized. Although she was baptized as a child in an Orthodox church, this time it was a believer's baptism as an adult, understanding the meaning and importance of it. Lucia was baptized with multiple garbage bags wrapped around her right foot because a week prior, she cut her tendons on glass in a field while running after Victoria who was running towards me. It looks like Satan tried to put different obstacles in our way, yet we still got baptized even while on crutches. On the same day of our baptism, our family and Jacob and Julia's family also from Moldova that came to St. John's after us, were accepted into the membership of First Baptist church.

We really appreciated the fellowship we had with other believers in St. John's and our wait for the Immigration hearing didn't seem to be as hard or cause as much psychological disturbance. But, as with anything unknowing for a human mind, the state of unknown expectation was in a way affecting my sleep. I can remember vividly the same dream over and over again, night after night: The Immigration officials came and took me to the airport and deported me back to Moldova. From there I was calling Pastor Mitchell and asking him to do something; maybe send a letter of invitation or an approval from Immigration so that I could get the visa and comeback to Canada. He would tell me the same thing each time I was calling him: "I can't do anything for you; I don't have any control over the Immigration". At that point, I would wake up without seeing the end of the dream, but surely thankful when saw my wife was sleeping next to me and realizing that this was just a dream. The last time I saw that dream was the night just before the hearing.

Chapter 18
My first car

    Finally I was able to find a part time job thanks to Slavic, a seaman who defected a year earlier from a ship that was refueling in St. John's harbor. He introduced me to the owner of a Greek pizzeria "No Name" who needed someone to deliver flyers between 10 a.m. and 3 p.m.; in hopes that in the afternoon and evening people would order pizza from his store.

    The boss would drive us to a certain area of St. Johns and give each one of us a map marked with a colored marker for the streets where he wanted us to push flyers. He liked us to put the flyer in the mailbox but leave 1/3 of it sticking out, so he could then drive around the streets we were working, and check if each house got the flyer. During the 5-6 months I was working there, he had many guys coming and going, either because they didn't like to walk too much, or they didn't do a good job and the boss asked them not to come anymore. On several occasions, just before taking us to the area, he would send one or two home, stating that he needed only 2 or 3 guys that day, but at times 5-6 guys would show up. I remember only once that I had to walk back home - about 2 km, because he had too many guys that day. I remember how I did not own the proper shoes to wear in the rainy weather, so Lucia bought a pair of boots from the Salvation Army, however they had a few holes in them. She would wrap two to three plastic bags from the grocery store around my feet so I would not get wet while delivering flyers.

So, the summer came and I was able to save a $1000.00. (Thanks to Lucia, who helped me in this endeavor - she did not spend any extra dollars when shopping because I was counting each receipt!) One evening she came back from Sobeys and when I calculated everything, she should have had over a dollar left in change. But she put only the small change in the piggybank and tried to hide the dollar. She saw a skirt she liked at the Salvation Army for six dollars, and when she went to do her weekly grocery store shopping, she planned to save a dollar to go towards buying the skirt. Lucia is thankful to this day for the kind ladies who were strangers driving on the road and would see Lucia walking on the sidewalk with bags in her hands and offer to bring her home. This kind gesture occurred almost every time she went to the grocery store until we purchased a car. Her plan of saving the dollar every week did not work! I needed that dollar for the car!! Lucia often brings up the memory of when I would come home from work on Fridays after getting paid. I would go to the suit in my closet where I kept the money I was saving for the car, and count the bills repeatedly, thinking they would have multiplied over the week.

As I looked through the daily local paper "The Telegram" one day I noticed this car; a 1987 Suzuki Forsa that was only $1200.00 I called the man and asked him if he would bring the car to our apartment and he came pretty fast. The deal was completed and in 10 minutes I became the proud owner of my first Canadian car. It took 9 months of waiting for this moment - the same as the length of a normal pregnancy! I thought my days of walking here and there had come to an end. I knew that there would be some expenses related to registration, plates, etc. but when I found out that my insurance would cost almost the same as the car because I was a new driver in Canada, my joy disappeared. I told my feet that it was not over yet. We decided to eat less, so that we could save more, and Lucia's favorite place at the grocery store became the clearance aisle, and the shopping mall was the Salvation Army. It did not take too long for me to finally register the car. The next morning when Lucia woke up and didn't see me there, she started to look for me, but I was nowhere to be found in our small apartment. She came outside and there I was, washing my car at 6 am. The overexcitement I had that morning kept me awake and I hate a dirty car!

Victoria in front of my shiny car

The boss noticed that I had a car and when I asked him about giving me a promotion from delivering flyers to delivering pizza he agreed. This was a real advancement in my career. My hourly wage went up 50 cents and I was making tips. Fortunately, my Suzuki had only 3 cylinders and a 1.0 cm3 engine, so I had some money left to bring home after filling up.

I can't stress enough the importance of having a car. On Wednesdays, the local businesses had a weekly paper called "Extra", and Terry, the manager would hire only those people who had a car. I would come at 9 p.m. and shuffle all the inserts, tighten them up in bundles of 50 papers, and around midnight, take them to a designated route. By 6:30 -7 a.m. people were expecting the Wednesday "Extra" in their mailboxes. Instead of going home and getting up early to deliver them, I would continue until 2:30-3 a.m. and finish them. Each week I had 150 to 200 papers, depending on the route. Then Halloween came, and one night (without any suspicions, and being very tired) I walked toward a mailbox and I saw a person standing there. It turned out to be a skeleton with sensor lights. You can imagine I got pretty scared!!!

Time passed by, day by day, and still there was no news from Immigration regarding our hearing date. Then Christmas came and what beautiful scenery everywhere. This was our second Christmas in Canada and Victoria was close to being 3 years old. After walking a good part of the day working, I would take her out in the evening to show her the houses with Christmas lights. I can still hear her saying "Wow, look at this one"!

Chapter 19
The hearing

The first two month of the New Year passed away uneventfully and here we are, arrived at March 1st, our hearing day. Pastor Mitchell has been visiting us couple of times per week to talk to us, encourage and pray for that day. He often will just point his finger up into the sky and say "Gospodi Bog, spasibo", which in translation from Russian means "Lord God, thank you". His knowledge of Russian was limited to a few basic words, but was using them faithfully.

Lucia chose a nice suit for me from a local men's store and I remember paying over $200 for it as the sales tax in Newfoundland were 19% at the time. It took us couple of months to pay for it. We decided that as professionals we needed to dress up, as one doesn't get the second chance to make the first impression. For her she got a cheap dress, but she looked nice in it.

We took Victoria to Jacob and Julia and drove to Water Street where the Immigration and Refugee board was located. At 8:30 am we were invited in the hearing room. There were several people there. On my right a Cuban man that served as a translator from Russian into English and back, next to him a lady from the Legal Aid services whose role was to introduce us before the judges, and act as an attorney, but in fact she wasn't able to do much. Just present there as required by protocol. On our left side an Immigration officer with big glasses and a thick folder in front of him full with material regarding Moldova. He has been collecting info on Moldova from the available sources at the time that may not been accurate, and were not reflecting the political and human rights situation in the country.

At 9 am two women entered the room. We heard from others that there is one woman judge by the name of Lisa G. but didn't know who the second one was. A voice announced: Please rise, the judges are here!

One of them greeted us and asked us to sit down, then pressed the recording's device button and said: Today is March 1, 1994. We are here to hear the case of Dr. and Mrs. Ivantchev, file number such and such… They started with me only for now.

During the interrogation process Lucia got a renal colic with severe pain in the back and left flank. Then, one of the judges wanted to stop the hearing, but she told them to continue. At that point the judge asked someone to bring couple of Tylenol and water and Lucia took the pills. The questions and answers went on for a few hours and judges decided that was time for lunch. After the lunch the recording device was turned on and the hearing continued with me. At 4:30 pm they said that my hearing will not be finished today and we should comeback on Thursday, which was in 2 days to finish my file and then start Lucia's.

Exhausted, we left the room and went to pick up Victoria from Jacob & Julia's place. They were curious to find out how the hearing was, but we couldn't tell much because it wasn't over yet. We were so tired that day that we went home and crushed.

In the morning, it was Wednesday, March 2nd, we got up and Lucia prepared the breakfast. Victoria was still in bed. I was drinking my coffee when the phone rang. I thought maybe is Pastor Mitchell calling to find out how the hearing went. But no, the call was from the Immigration and Refugee Board. Good morning, this is Joan D. calling; I would like to speak with Sergei. This is Sergei I replied.

"Sergei, the Immigration board listened to tape recorder this morning and they decided to give you a refugee status in Canada". Congratulations. You don't have to come to Thursday hearing, but

Lucia will have her hearing as scheduled, if she wants to have the same status. I was standing when she told me that and the joy and excitement almost caused me to drop off my coffee. Lucia was sitting on my right side and watching me and not getting what is happening. I can see vividly her curious face even today.

After telling the lady on the other end that I'll discuss with my wife about her plans, I hang up.

What happened? Who called you? - asked Lucia. I had to tell her 'Welcome to Canada"!

Wonderful news, great, thank God is over. We were extremely happy that moment.

But, you need to go for your hearing on Thursday I told her. No, I am not going through what we went through yesterday. I'll leave Canada and return based on the family reunification act, but not going to the hearing.

We had to go to Immigration office and let them know that Lucia and Victoria will leave Canada. According to the law of that time she needed to show a stamp of a foreign country in her passport to prove to the officials that she officially left Canada, entered a different country, and returned back to Canada because her husband was accepted there officially.

The closest country to Newfoundland was the islands of Saint Pierre and Miquelon, a French territory just off the coast of Newfoundland. The provincial airlines were flying there and the flight time was only 40 minutes one way. We had to borrow $500 from friends in order to purchase 2 round trip tickets for Lucia and Victoria.

A few days later I took them to St. John's airport and waited there for them to comeback with a French visa in her passport. Victoria did not have her own, but was included in Lucia's. The total trip took only 3 hrs. They entered Canada on a different status, as independent immigrants.

Now we can breathe easy, no more doubts about what was going to happen to us, etc.

My nightly dream prior to hearing has never repeated itself. At times I wanted to get it again to see what would happen, but don't recall seeing it ever again.

What a relief, like a heavy burden was lifted up. We realized that God was in control over our destiny and had all prepared for us. But humanly speaking, we had worries and doubts. This was another sign for us to grow in faith and trust God in all we do, knowing that if God is for us, no one can be against us. That is what the Scripture says. I know it's true.

Cabot Tower; St. John's, NFLD

Chapter 20
What's next?

Now that the Immigration status was solved, I started to think about more serious work than the pizza store. Jerry and Sue a couple from church organized a small party for us to celebrate our acceptance into Canada. We had a nice time together that evening. Victoria ate a huge peace of cake is a shape of a lamb. We remembered the first time we attended their church and couldn't speak anything more than "My name is" or "I don't speak English", and the time I started to attend choir practices and couldn't read the words and follow the notes the same time.

Dona, our English teacher offered to go with me to the Newfoundland Medical board to find out what I needed to do so I could practice in Canada. At the board I was told that they don't need any foreign physicians because there are very limited opportunities for them in Canada. They told me that will need to take the Medical Council of Canada examinations, but even if I pass these exams I'll not be able to find a residency position to complete the postgraduate training in order to get the license. Now, looking back I see the poor judgment used in decision making process toward the foreign physicians. If in the mid 1990's the government accepted us, Canada would end up today having a shortage of family physicians. At that time I was out of active practice for just little over a year, and if this was today, I could qualify for a 6 month assessment period which is in place now. But, this wasn't the case and I needed to make a decision what to do next.

I went to Memorial University to look for other opportunities in health care field and was offered a volunteer work in the Emergency Department. This turned out to be beneficial in one hand as I was pushing stretchers to X-ray and back, taking the urine sample to lab, etc. Exposure to the Emergency department work and patients, speaking the medical language, it helped me gain a first hand experience in a hospital environment. At the other hand it didn't help me in any way put bread on the table. At the end of the week there was no paycheck coming home. So, I went to see if I could get an evaluation of my Physician Assistant diploma, and got the same answer. There are no PAs in the public health care, except a few opportunities in the military.

As the summer came and days got longer, we had more time to spend outside with other friends and families. During one of the discussions Andrei and Enna told us that they are moving to Ottawa in July. He already has been in Toronto to visit a friend and didn't feel moving there, but heard good things about Ottawa. From Toronto Andrei brought a newspaper where he red about a Green Card Lottery in the United States, but couldn't understand all the details. So we spend some time reading it over and realized that it was free of charge and that once a year the State Department gives out about 50,000 immigrant visas to qualified applicants. I told him that I am going to apply, so he did as well. I applied for myself, another letter for Lucia to increase the chance, then for each member of our families, parents, brothers, sisters. I remember sending out 11 letters. But, we didn't know what address to leave for the Department of State to contact us in case we win the lottery, because we also were thinking about moving from St. John's. I decided to leave my parents address in Moldova.

In July we left St. John's for Ottawa. At the last Sunday service pastor Whiteside gave us a nice album with beautiful pictures taken by one of the men from church with a farewell note. Early morning the trip began. We where the first car of this official cortège, Jacob & Julia in the middle, and Andrei & Enna the last car. As soon as we exited the city two moose stopped in the middle of the highway and would not move. It was early morning and somewhat foggy and probably they were not completely awake. I pressed the brake immediately and clonk a few times, but no movement. Then she went away, but he had huge horns and looked at us for a few seconds, then walked slowly into the woods. In front of us laid a distance of approximately 3000 km. Good bye Newfoundland.

Chapter 21
Welcome to Ottawa

Our journey to Ottawa had a few wrong turns to put it literally. After a night on the ferry sleeping on the floor because it was too expensive to get a cabin on the ferry from Newfoundland to Nova Scotia, the next morning it was foggy and our only direction came from a map from Pastor Mitchell. Lucia and I were in one car, along with two other families in two other cars following us. I took a wrong turn at a rotary and the other families were upset with my driving mistake. I remember telling them that they should go ahead and lead the way then, but no one wanted to. We spent another night in a motel near Edmundston NB, I remember Victoria asking us where our house is because at this point it was taking us three days and different sleeping locations to arrive at our destination. I told Victoria jokingly that our house was in the car at this point. We arrived in Ottawa the next afternoon. I had only a simple map with me, as GPS wasn't invented at that time, and I was looking for an exit to Bank Street. According to our map there was supposed to be a canal first, (the Rideau Canal) and then Bank Street; but I couldn't see the canal because it runs under highway 417 and cannot be seen from the highway. We were told by other people who had left Newfoundland that when families arrive in Ottawa, they go to the Bank Street YMCA and get a very cheap room until a suitable apartment can be found. As we were driving through the city on 417 there were no signs for Bank Street. Shortly we arrived at Moody Drive exit, which is in the west end of the city. I pulled over, as did Jacob and Andrei who were following me. I got out of the car and stopped a car driving by. When the guy saw our Newfoundland plates, he started laughing, but he didn't mind explaining how to get to the YMCA. I turned around and followed the gentleman's directions.

At the YMCA they sent us to Murray Street for temporary accommodations. We got a room that had a double bed and a small single one for Victoria. This was a downgrade for us compared to the St. John's apartment, but we were thankful for it. Pastor Mitchell gave us a phone number of a local pastor and I called him two days later. He was very helpful to us in getting an apartment, as we didn't have many references, or a job in Ottawa. He co-signed for our one year lease, and we moved to Banner Road. Fortunately, all three families got apartments in the same building and started to attend Haven Baptist Church which was only about five km distance away.

Ottawa is a pretty nice city, and very green in the summer. I started the search for a job. The classified section of Ottawa Citizen became my daily reading. I applied at a tool company, and at a couple of nursing homes, but got no calls back so I went to my old job for which I had Canadian experience - a pizza store. The owner was an Afghani man. Initially he said that he didn't need anyone for delivery, but could give me a few hours per week to work inside. So I learned quickly how to make fresh dough, cut the onions and tomatoes, make boxes, deliver flyers, etc. I remember how one of the men from church joked (in a nice way) about my job, saying "If you can't deliver babies then deliver pizza". Not too long after, I actually started delivering pizza. The tips in Ottawa were better than I had been getting in St. John's, but I can't say the same thing about the taste of the pizza.

In September I enrolled in a basic computer class at St. Andrew's school where they taught us typing as well. I passed the test requirement by typing a minimum 20 words per minute using only 2 fingers, but I didn't have time to learn DOS applications. At that point I decided to take some English classes to improve my grammar.

By this time, Lucia and Victoria had been waiting for almost 2 years to go and visit her family. Because they were immigrants, and not a refugee as I was, they were able to leave and come back into Canada without any problems. We got the tickets and Lucia and Victoria went to Moldova for 8 weeks. The journey back to Moldova took four day, when it should have taken only 24 hours. They were supposed to fly from Montreal to Bucharest, with a stop in Prague. Instead, they ended up in Bratislava because of the foggy weather. From there, they were put on a bus and taken to Prague. From Prague, they flew us to Budapest, and finally they were put in a hotel. Lucia and Victoria were so happy to finally take a shower after four days of travel. In the morning they flew from Budapest to Bucharest, where Lucia's brother Ivan was waiting for her for five days to arrive. It took another six hours to arrive home in Moldova from there. This was the longest time I had been alone since getting married. I worked most of the days at the pizza store, and studied at home for the medical exams. One day Vasile, a Moldovan friend living in Ottawa at that time, came over to teach me how to make borshch. Before, I didn't like to cook, and I thought it would be difficult to learn the skill, but it was pretty easy. I guess it makes it easier when you have a good instructor.

While Lucia and Victoria were in Moldova, my dad called me regarding a "large white envelope" that he had received with my name on it. I asked him, "Where did it come from?" He couldn't tell me exactly because was in English, but he told me that it had a stamp on it "U.S. Air Mail". I asked him to have my mom read the address on it, etc. and she said that it was from the Department of State. Immediately I felt it inside of me that it was the Green Card Lottery notification that I had applied for almost a year earlier in Newfoundland. I told her, "Mom this is good news! I'll be able to get permanent residency in the U.S. and sponsor you to come to the U.S. as well."

Starting in the late 1980's, the U.S. congress had adopted a law initiated by President Reagan, which allowed former Soviet citizens who were Christians during the regime, and had suffered persecution because of their faith; the opportunity to apply through the U.S. Embassy in Moscow to be considered refugees in the U.S. One of the conditions was that these applicants must have a first-degree relative living in the U.S. to act as a sponsor when they arrive. The government would provide them with a small stipend and food stamps for the first 6-7 months; but their relatives needed to find them an apartment and assist them with a job search, etc. I felt God's hand in all of this, and the passage from the scriptures came to mind about when Joseph was sold by his brothers to the Egyptians as a slave, but God turned it for good, and Joseph was able to help his family later on when famine came over Israel. This situation spoke to me over and over again, assuring me that God was in control of our lives and that we needed to trust Him.

I asked my mom to give the envelope to Lucia so that she could read all the instructions and prepare the necessary paperwork for our Green Card interview. The State Department was asking us to provide letters from Moldova that we had not been convicted of any criminal offenses, and that we had enough money to live in the U.S. for minimum of one year without becoming a public charge. As I remember, at that time for a family of three, Immigration asked that we provide a bank statement with $19,000 minimum balance in order to qualify.

Guess what I prepared the day Lucia and Victoria returned from Moldova? Yes, it was borshch! They liked it so much that I had to prepare it again on a different occasion, but not since. If they would ask me today to make it, probably I'd have to call Vasile again.

Chapter 22
Green Card

Lucia brought the necessary papers from Moldova, and we started to put together the file for the Green Card interview. Although I was working at the pizza place, it would have taken me years to save the minimum $19,000 required to show at the interview, so I borrowed money from several friends and deposited it in my bank account to reach the balance required. Also, one of the conditions was to provide an employment offer in the US in the form of a letter, and bring it to the interview at the Embassy. I contacted Victor, a friend from Moldova who was living in Massachusetts and working for a trucking company to see if they need truck drivers. About a week later I received a letter from Schneider's that they need drivers and would offer me a job.

We had all the educational papers translated, got all the letters from the police department and bank, and went for the interview at the U.S. Consulate General in Toronto. The first day we spent at a clinic in downtown Toronto getting blood work, X-rays, and physical exams. The second day we were expected to go to the Consulate. That day they called other applicants as well, so the waiting area was full. Every one was talking different languages, but a couple sitting not far from us were speaking Bulgarian, so we talked with them a little bit as they spoke some Russian.

The interviewer was sitting behind a glass window and the applicant sat on the other side. We could not hear what they were asking, but when this Bulgarian family went to be interviewed, I could hear him saying "It was required for my job to be a member of the communist party." Then he responded to another question - I don't remember what he answered, but it appeared that the interviewer had asked him why he had enrolled in the communist party, or something similar to that, and he was defending himself. At that point I looked at Lucia, and she looked at me, and we were somewhat puzzled about the interview process. We didn't know for sure how it would go, because the State Department had notified 100,000 applicants around the world that year, and only 50,000 green cards were available. So, every second person was excluded at the interview time - or for some of them, the criminal background check would not be cleared, etc. One thing we knew - that if it was God's will for us to get it, He would work it out. Also we were not members of the communist party, and our background check should return clear.

Our turn came, and we had a lady interviewing us. As she was looking through the papers, she noticed that I was a physician and said; ***"O, you will do well in the U.S. as a physician."*** She probably noticed that I did not have a license to practice in Canada or the U.S., but was satisfied with the education alone. Then she saw the employment offer, and looked at me, but didn't say anything at that time. In a few minutes she asked us to come into a different room where she took our fingerprints. I can see her clearly even now rolling my fingers over the pad and asking me ***"What is there in common between medicine and truck driving?"*** I told her that my goal was to go through the process and obtain the medical license, but in case that did not work, I didn't mind working as a truck driver. She seemed satisfied with the answer and didn't ask us any other questions. At the end of the interview she told us to wait for the notification in the mail to come back for the immigrant visa when the background check was received.

Feeling happy about the interview process, we drove back to Ottawa.

Chapter 23
Welcome to United States

A few months later we received a letter to come to Toronto for the immigrant visa. When we arrived there, the Consulate officer took us into a room and handed us a yellow envelope. It was quite large and heavy. He reminded us repeatedly not to open it, and said that we have 3 months to cross the U.S. border and surrender this unopened envelope to the immigration officials there.

Now the question was… "Where were we going?!"

We were supposed to tell the officers when we crossed the border, the address that we were moving to in the U.S., so that our Green Cards could be sent there. Again, I contacted my friend Victor who was working as a truck driver, and he told me to come to Pittsfield, a nice city in western Massachusetts. He had been there for three years already, and felt that we would like it there as well. I told him that I would contact him a day or two before we would be crossing the border, and confirm his address.

However, a couple of weeks later when I called my parents in Moldova, my dad told me that one of my class mates also lived in Massachusetts, in a town named Greenfield. He gave me her phone number and I called her the same day. She was so glad I called because she had been in the U.S. only 6 months, and knew that I was in Canada, but she didn't know how to find me. When I told her that we had won the Green Card Lottery and needed to provide an address to immigration officials when crossing the border, she didn't think have to think much. "Come to Greenfield...you'll like it, I promise! It is very green!" she said.

One July morning we decided to go. All three of us got in the car and drove to the Cornwall border crossing, about 100 km from Ottawa. We crossed the bridge over the St. Lawrence River and arrived at U.S. Customs and Immigration. The officer asked us where we lived and where we were going - standard procedure; but when he saw that we had the yellow envelope, he asked us to come inside. There, another officer looked long after me, and then asked where we were going to stay in the U.S. I told him that initially we would stay with my friend, a former classmate from Moldova. Then he asked, "Where is your stuff? I told him that everything else was in Ottawa - we were going to see the area, and process the Green Card papers at the same time. He replied, "Oh no...you go back to Ottawa! Get all your stuff first, and then move to U.S." He was swinging his arms and pointing north toward Ottawa, and then south toward Massachusetts. So, we did a 180 degree U turn and went back to Canada.

We could not believe what he had told us. I thought he was joking, but no, he was dead serious. He would not allow us into the U.S. Period!

We crossed the bridge back into Canada and Lucia said that we should go back to Ottawa because Victoria had started to get a fever. I stopped at a walk-in clinic in Cornwall to see a physician, thankful that the OHIP card worked all over the country. He told us that she probably had a virus, and to give her Tylenol and fluids and she would get better. I knew that myself, but needed confirmation from a licensed physician, not a pizza delivery doctor.

At that time I said we should try a different border crossing, and that going back to the Cornwall crossing was not an option. There were no cell phones at that time, and Melanie was waiting for us to arrive in about 7-8 hours. I looked at the map, and saw that there were two more border crossings in Ontario, and several in Quebec. I decided to go through Montreal and cross into Vermont where Hwy 89 begins. In about three hours we were at the border again. Here the officer asked us about the documents, and I gave him that yellow envelope. He told me to park the car and come inside. We went into a room where a gray haired officer was at a desk, and behind him on the wall were pictures of President Clinton and Secretary of State Warren Christopher. That officer was pretty nice and didn't get into much detail. He saw that we had all the paperwork in order, and it seemed insignificant to him how much stuff we had, or didn't have. He took me first for fingerprinting. Although we had done it at the Consulate in Toronto, the border officer told us that all three of us need to be fingerprinted again. He did well with me and Lucia, but when Victoria's turn came, she was only 4 years old and her tiny fingers were bending all over that pad, but he seemed to be able to accomplish the entrusted task. After that, he stamped our Red Soviet passports with a stamp, and stated that we were admitted for one year, and that usually within that year, the Green Card would come in the mail. Then he shook our hands and said, "Welcome to the United States." It sounded very nice, as he was smiling at us.

In 3.5 hrs we arrived in Greenfield, and found Melanie's address pretty easily. Indeed, Greenfield was green, but so was everything else around, especially the drive down through Vermont. What a picture site.

We stayed a couple of days in Greenfield, went to Route 63 for a shashlik, visited Melanie's parents, and had a good time overall.

However, my Afghani boss was waiting for me back in Ottawa to make dough and cut vegetables.

Chapter 24
Moldova visit

After working hard for two months, I decided that it was time to see my parents. It had been almost three years since we had left Moldova, and Lucia and Victoria had gone there the year before, so it was my turn. We didn't have enough money to travel all together at the same time.

I arrived at night in Bucharest, Romania which was the closest city to my parent's home, which had a direct flight from Montreal. At that time my brother was studying in Timisoara, where the 1989 revolution started. He came to meet me at the Otopeni airport and with him was Valera, my close friend and classmate from medical school. Valera had driven from Chisinau to meet me, and take me to my parents, which was about 600 km northeast of Bucharest.

As we left the airport and drove about 4-5 km and immediately two police cars pushed us to the shoulder of the road and surrounded our car. The officers got out of their cars and pointed their guns toward us yelled very loudly in Romanian; "Out of the car, keep your hands behind your back and don't move." For a moment it felt like we were in a movie, but they were serious. My brother tried to tell them that he was a student there, and had just met me at the airport, and we were going to a hotel. They didn't want to listen much, so I explained that I had just arrived from Canada, and this was my friend from Moldova, and my brother with him. One of them said; "I know what you people from Moldova are doing here - stealing cars." Valera had a VAZ 2106 model with Moldovan plates, and they probably thought this car was just stolen. Another officer got in the car and searched it, opened the hood, looked at the technical passport, the engine's number, VIN, etc. After one of them checked my Canadian travel document, they left us alone and explained that many cars have being stolen in Bucharest by guys from Moldova, and they had just gotten a description of a stolen car similar to Valera's. We drove to a hotel, and in the morning left for Moldova. At the Romanian border check the lady officer looked at me and said, "You are so lucky you live in Canada. How did you get there?" I told her that was a long story.

We were driving on the bridge over the Prut River and the Moldovan border check point were in less than 300 meters. I discussed with Valera that, if he was asked, to tell the border officials that he was bringing me back home from my brother's in Timisoara. I didn't want to mention anything about Canada - it would have just complicated things to an unknown result. I still had my red ex- Soviet passport with the stamp that I was a citizen of Moldova, and even though Moldova had issued new blue passports already, many people still used their old Soviet style passports until their expiration. As the officer checked our passports, I complimented him that the crossing point looked nice and clean. It had only been open for about three years and I had never driven through that one before. He asked Valera to open the trunk. There was nothing else in there except my luggage, so he let us enter into Moldova without any hassle. In about 100 km I would reach my parents' house and eat a good lunch, borshch also included.

A couple of days later I went to my old work place in Chisinau and everyone were happy to see me. The chief asked if I would do a locum while there. I agreed to do it and the next day I went to the OR. One of my colleagues, Victor, was still working there. I started my first case, a 44 year old woman having a hysterectomy. Katya was my nurse that day and she administered the pre-medication as ordered, checked all the vitals with a manual blood pressure cuff, and pushed the induction dose of anesthetic. I was holding the mask with 100% Oxygen on, and waiting until the patient was asleep to administer the muscle relaxants to intubate the trachea. As Katya pushed the relaxant dose and I intubated the trachea, I saw that patient's color was turning blue. I listened to the lungs - good respiration's bilaterally. I rechecked the tube placement; it was in the right place, going through the vocal cords. The hospital had only one portable pulse oximetry and it was used in a Cesarean section room, but the ventilators were basic volume controlled without ECG or capnography tracings. I asked Katya to give the patient a few blows with the Ambu bag while I checked the machine to see what was happening. As soon as she bagged the patient a few times, her color improved. When I turned back to the machine to check the circuit, I noticed that the oxygen flow meter was turned off; and nitrous oxide meter fully open. Victor was standing next to the machine and smiling in a sarcastic way. "I just wanted to check how vigilant you are after not giving anesthesia for almost three years". He admitted that he had turned the oxygen off and cranked the nitrous oxide up, but he would have reversed it if I hadn't figured things out in a short time. Certainly I didn't appreciate that, and told him that a behavior like that would result in a disciplinary action in Canada.

I enjoyed the rest of my visit there, and three weeks went by pretty fast. During that time, I experienced a closed fracture of my 4th metacarpal bone, compliments of Lucia's brother Ivan, during a special handshake maneuver. But all the nice visits with parents, relatives and friends made me feel at home. However, it was time to return to Ottawa, where my real family was waiting for me.

Chapter 25
Me becoming an RN, and Lucia a cosmetologist

Time was flying fast. We had lived in Canada for over three years and nothing had changed in regards to my professional career. I tried the USMLE Step 1 exam, which was a basic sciences exam and I failed it. It was so difficult, full of biochemistry and pathology questions that I had studied in the middle of the 80's. I couldn't believe how I had gotten even a 61, but the passing score was 75. I said to myself, "I need to do something in order to get back into the medical profession.

Anna, who had been a nurse in Moldova and had moved with us from St. John's to Ottawa, found out that the College of Nurses of Ontario had started a refresher program that year. It was for nurses who had been out of practice for 5 years or longer, or who had let their licenses expire and now needed a refresher to be eligible to write the exam again. I drove to Toronto and met with a College representative. She looked through my papers and diplomas and told me that she could not consider my medical education from Moldova, but she could look through the curriculum I had in the Physician Assistant program. I returned to Ottawa not knowing what her decision would be, but hoping that she would allow me to take the refresher program. A few weeks later I got a letter stating that there were no PAs in Canada, but the College would accept most of the curriculum from Moldova, and, if I wanted to become a Registered Nurse, they would allow me to enroll in that refresher program. So I did.

The classes were scheduled to start in September. Until then I was working at the pizza restaurant. One day I found an ad in the paper asking for a person with medical knowledge to take care of a quadriplegic patient. I called him to inquire about it and he started asking me questions - like did I know what a C5-C6 injury was. I told him that I had an idea and he asked me to fax him my resume. When he read it, he called the next day and asked me to come and see how the other male caregiver took care of him. To my surprise, the other man was a Russian immigrant, "Ilya", who had lived in Ottawa for a couple of years. My patient was a famous Canadian skier who had injured himself in the mid 80's in England jumping from a trampoline. He was a nice guy, but because of his life circumstances, he had become very bitter and cranky at times. I worked 3 or 4 days a week and Ilya worked the other 3 or 4 days. The patient lived in downtown Ottawa in a nice wheelchair-accessible apartment designed for people with injuries like his. GM had built him a Chevy Blazer that he was able to drive even though he was quadriplegic. He had very little movement in his left arm, and some movements of the fingers in the right hand. The door opened remotely and a ramp would come out of the car so he could get in it with his wheelchair. I remember one day driving with him on the 417 and he was passing other cars, driving in the left lane at times, it was scary. That was my first and last time driving with him on the highway.

My patient's routine started at 6 a.m. with me going slowly into the apartment and waking him up. Then I emptied the leg bag, lifted him up, dressed and transferred him into the wheelchair. Then I wheeled him into the bathroom, shaving him at times, though usually this was done during the night routine. After I washed his face, he brushed his teeth with an automated brush, using his left hand. After this, came the hair-do moment. At times this could take twenty minutes or more. His hair was long and needed brushing and drying with the help of a hairdryer; always in a certain way, and this changed every day - even several times per morning. If he didn't like it he would tell me, *"**Not this way, this way**!"* by moving his head in one direction or the other – meaning that was the direction he wanted the hair to be brushed and dried. Then breakfast consisted of cereal or oatmeal and coffee. After that I dressed him for work and / or social events. He would leave the house around 8 - 8:15 a.m.

The evening routine was longer: I was to come at 8 pm after he had dinner. (he had people who just prepared his food, but I never saw them.) Firstly, he bathed in the bathtub (by candlelight) while I washed his hair and body, and shaved him. To get him to and from the tub, I needed to carry him in my arms. Getting him out was hardest because he was all wet. Therefore, he needed strong man to take care of him. My back didn't appreciate the abuse, but the hourly wage he paid me was twice as much as I was making at the pizza store. After the bath, I dried him with big towels, combed his hair and proceeded with his bowel procedure which would take at least 30 - 45 minutes. Details omitted.

So, mornings and evenings I worked as a private duty attendant; and during the day I helped Lucia clean houses. Sometimes I had to take some kidding from a friend questioning why I was doing this. "Did you come to Canada to clean someone else's shit?" he asked me. I told him that someone needed to do that, and it happened to be my wife and myself. We knew this was just temporary.

I worked for this patient the whole summer, mornings and evenings. When my nursing program started in September I had to resign, because his morning routine took too long would make me late for classes.

It was at this time that Lucia also decided to go to Marvel Beauty School of Cosmetology in 1995. She had discovered that she liked making people look nice. With a Technologist degree in perfume and cosmetics, she had never had to cut hair before coming to Canada. When we were in Newfoundland she had started to cut my hair and she used to practice on me with big scissors she found at the dollar store. We could not afford to continuously pay $10 for a haircut, so

Lucia wanted to give it a try and save money at the same time. She got so good at it, our friend Andrei would regularly come to our place for a haircut as well! She realized it would give her joy and personal satisfaction when school was over and she was licensed to work with real clients. She would go to school in the morning, then she would go after school to her house cleaning job in the afternoon. She did this for an entire year until she graduated.

A few days after starting my program, a different man asked me if I could help with another quadriplegic. I was referred to him by my first client. The second patient, named Pierre, was a French Canadian who was much older than the first client, but his routines were simpler. Pierre had been working at the Canadian Consulate in Boston, and one day when he was driving his Toyota Celica from Boston to Ottawa, he was in an accident and became quadriplegic. He was a very sweet and interesting man. I took care of him through my nursing school year and for several more months after graduating until we moved to the USA.

During this time, I saw how blessed I was to be healthy, to have a nice family, and to be restarting my professional career. I would not take for granted what I had in my life, but would give thanks to God for everything. Lessons of humility I learned while taking care of these two patients will stay with me throughout life.

Chapter 26
My parents' arrival

Because I now had the Green Card, I was able to apply to sponsor my parents to come to the United States. The U.S. Congress had adopted a law allowing former Soviet citizens who had been persecuted because of their religion, to come to the U.S. if they had a first degree relative already living there, who could act as their sponsor.

After filling out all the necessary paperwork, my parents, my brother Victor, and his wife, as well as my sister Viorica were invited for an interview at the U.S. Embassy in Moscow. For some reason, the immigration officials decided to appoint my mom as the principal applicant, so at the interview, the officer mostly asked about her experiences as a Christian living in the Soviet Union. My dad had much more to say, but whenever he wanted to help my mom, the officers got angry and asked him to sit quietly. By the end of the day everyone had passed the interview. Six months later they received their papers and the okay to move to the U.S. we already had an apartment in Greenfield for them that was furnished as much as we could so they can have their basic needs for their beginning of a new life in America. We went from Ottawa to New York to meet them at the JFK airport. Lucia, and Melanie (my classmate and friend from Greenfield), and her husband Chirita also came. Lucia was about 28 weeks pregnant with our second child. My parents flew here with Delta Airlines from Moscow, and arrived on time.

After they passed through Immigration and Customs, and their entrance papers were processed, I saw them far away coming through a long hall. Victor was pushing a large cart and was in the lead. My sister was dressed in a long black coat and a black hat, and I did not even see her until she jumped from the side to hug me. Finally, my dad and mom came. As we were greeting, hugging and kissing, Chirita was video recording the whole reunion, and at the same time talking like a reporter. He likes to talk in real life and did a good job that day.

We went to Greenfield, and everyone moved into my apartment, which had been empty just waiting for them to arrive. All were jet lagged and tired. The time was after 10 PM, but we ate supper, and Melanie gave each one of them a small gift as a welcome gesture. We went to bed after midnight. Victoria wanted to be with Grandma in bed, so that Grandma could sing to her and massage her back. My mom was tired, but Victoria liked this so much that she would not let her sleep. She remembered how Grandma had sung to her when she had visited Moldova twice since moving to Canada. I am sure if asked, she would know the songs by heart even today at nineteen years of age.

We had to stay a couple of days in Greenfield to help them apply for Social Security Numbers, as well as other business related with a new immigrant arrival. Although we wanted to stay longer, we had to go because I was in nursing school, Victoria was in kindergarten, and Lucia was working at Magic Cuts at the Bank Street Mall. She had graduated before me and was now the breadwinner in the family. Even today, she is my personal hairdresser, barber, you name it. In over 28 years no one else has touched my coiffure. "I love my stylist".

Chapter 27
Welcome Nicole

March arrived, and Victoria's and my dad's birthdays were approaching. At this point Lucia was about 32-33 weeks pregnant. I don't know what I was thinking at that time, but I am sure I was not thinking like a doctor. (I guess I can make the argument that I did not have a license to practice medicine in Canada.) Anyway, as International Woman's Day was coming to an end, I told Lucia, "Tomorrow is Sunday - let's surprise my dad on his birthday and drive down to Massachusetts." Victoria was on school break, and I had only one class the following Monday, so we could be back in time for my Tuesday clinical at Riverside Hospital. Lucia's pregnancy was going well, and she was still working 3-4 days per week, but she didn't feel like driving in the car for six hours. That week I had purchased for my dad a 1990 Sonata for $1200.00 Canadian. That would be equal to about $850-900 U.S., and Victor hadn't been able to find anything there for this amount, so I felt I had another reason to go, and deliver the car. Lucia told me to go ahead with Victoria, and she would stay in Ottawa, but I insisted she come. I am at times stubborn, I have to admit. We left around noon and arrived in Greenfield in time for supper and birthday cake. The trip was fine. Victoria played with Grandpa, riding on his back, and we made funny video episodes; then we all went to bed.

Around 4:30 a.m. Lucia woke me up saying, "Look, I am wet! "I think my water broke." I replied, "Don't worry, it's probably nothing; maybe you coughed during your sleep and your bladder let go a few drops…Sleep…"

At 6:30 she woke me again, saying, "I am wet this time for sure!" I said, "Okay, let me check." When I touched the bed sheets, I could see they were soaked. "Yes," I said, "it looks like your water broke." I was thinking, "What are we going to do? To drive to the Quebec border is a minimum of three to three and a half hours away, and we don't have insurance to go to local hospital here." Finally, I decided we had to go to Franklin Medical Center, which is only two miles from where my parents lived. Close to eight a.m. we arrived at the hospital, and at the registration desk I told them that we were from Canada, and that we didn't have insurance. The clerk said that we shouldn't worry about this because they had similar situations in the past, and that Canadian insurance would pay the bill. "Okay," I said. She sent us to the third floor, where labor and delivery was located. A midwife was on call, and the obstetrician was on back up if needed. She checked Lucia and said that she had indeed broken her water, but was not in labor yet. However, she suggested that we not leave the hospital. So we stayed. The real labor started after five p.m. and near seven-thirty p.m. a 2 kg (4 lbs 10 oz) girl was born at 33 weeks. I had worked in the maternity hospital in the past, and was used to newborns, but this tiny, small one was mine. That was a different feeling. I remember calling Lucia's mom to share the good news that she would have another granddaughter and she told me that Lucia was born seven months premature. When my mom came to see Nicole, she was worried because the baby was so small, but I remember that Lucia herself was born at seven months, and weighed 1.9 kg. Everyone was surprised to hear that Lucia and Nicole share this in common, and we felt more assured that the baby would be fine.

I wanted to pick a name for her, but we didn't know which one to choose. Since I had chosen Victoria's name, this time it was Lucia's turn. She wanted Anastasia, Ekaterina, Nicoleta, etc. I asked what the midwife's name was and she said it was Beth. So I told Lucia, "Maybe we can call her Elizabeth?" But Lucia said she would call her Nicole, for Nicoleta. Then I suggested calling her Elizabeth for her middle name and she agreed. I think she was tired and did not want to argue with me. And so, "Nicole Elizabeth" was born on March 10th. Lucia was not prepared to have a baby in the United States because all of the items that were prepared for the newborn baby was left in Canada. The second day after Lucia delivered the baby, she went to Walmart to buy all the necessary items for Nicole to have while in Massachusetts. Now we would start celebrating the 8th of March for International Women's Day, the 9th as Victoria's birthday, and the 10th Nicole's. That means in February I have to work extra hours to generate the cash for my girls.

Nicole stayed in the hospital for five or six days because her bilirubin was elevated and she required light blankets and frequent blood draws. On the way to Greenfield, we had come with the car I'd purchased for my dad, so my brother was supposed to take us up to the U.S. / Canadian border, and our friend Pedro from Ottawa would take us into Canada. My brother couldn't cross the border because he did not have his Green Card yet, since they had only been in the U.S. one month. I called Pedro to come to Ogdensburg, the closest border crossing – Ogdensburg, only seventy-five km. from Ottawa. On the way from Greenfield, we drove into a snowstorm near Watertown, NY and we couldn't see anything ahead of us. We thought that Pedro would leave because we were running late…remember – we had no cell phones in those days. But when we got to the border there he was, waiting for us, thank God. We moved from one car to another, and went back to Ottawa one hour later with an American girl in the car seat.

We left a family of three, and came home four.

Chapter 28
My nursing career begins

After completing the classroom curriculum, I started my clinical practicum.

My obstetrical practicum was at Riverside Hospital. Each morning before the shift began, a pregnant patient would be assigned to me, and I was responsible for her care during that shift. The clinical instructor would check to see if we needed help, but most of the questions were addressed by the charge nurse. One day, the patient assigned to me delivered with some difficulties, and the baby required extra oxygen, and bag mask ventilation. There was only the obstetrician, a nurse from the floor, and a nurse from the nursery in the delivery room. The pediatric nurse started to dry the baby, and stimulate him, but the baby was not showing any signs of breathing independently, so I took the neonatal Ambu bag and started to bag the newborn. The OBS doctor thought I was from respiratory therapy and did not interfere with my resuscitation efforts. However, the baby needed intubation, and I wanted to do that, but the pediatric nurse called the anesthesiologist. I had intubated newborns many times in the past, but in this situation, I was just a student nurse. I did not realize that there might be consequences. It didn't take very long for my clinical instructor to arrive, and then the lecture started. "Do you realize what will be on the front page of Ottawa Citizen Newspaper tomorrow? "Student Nurse Intubates a newborn" She said, "Even if it was done appropriately and successfully, this is not a part of your skill. Is that clear??!!" I said, "Yes, I get it."

Until that time, no one knew that I had been an anesthesiologist in Moldova. When this fact became known to the med-surgery clinical instructor, my nightmares began. It seemed she didn't like guys for some reason; and now, with me, she had a male ex-doctor under her authority. Her attitude became, "Okay, let me show him what I can do!!" I remember how she screamed at me one day at the Civic Hospital, "Sergei!! Forget that you were a doctor!", "Go and get that bed pan!", "I'll flunk you!", and "You'll not pass my course!" etc. I had to work extra hard to please her, and I was so happy when this part of my training was over and graduation day came.

The RN exam which was administered by the College of Nurses of Ontario, wasn't until May or June, so for a month or two after graduation I could work as a graduate nurse. That was a bad time in the healthcare field, and very few nursing jobs were available. I was hired to do only part time work as a night-shift sitter on the psych ward at the Civic Hospital. Even having an RN license did not help getting a full time position, so I thought about moving to the U.S. at that point. I needed only to write the NCLEX exam, and I could get the license and a job because I already had the Green Card.

The timing worked well in our favor. We had applied for Canadian citizenship over six months prior to this, and in May we were called to go for the citizenship exam. This exam included one history part, and one part about knowledge of the Canadian government and its' structure. I remember getting one or two wrong out of all the questions. I don't remember for sure how many questions were on that test, but we had prepared from a book with over 200 questions.

We were called to go to the citizenship ceremony on the 30th of May. I can remember all the details about that day. In one word, it was "awesome!" The judge entered the large auditorium where there were probably over 100 people. She mentioned that 36 countries were represented in that room. Moldova was one of them. We all got up and sang the national anthem "O Canada." Then she spoke for 10-

15 minutes, giving a very touching and personal speech. She said things like "You are Canadians now. This is your country to love and to cherish, to work for, and defend. Wherever you go in the world, remember, Canada is waiting for you. You are, and always will be, welcomed back."

Ironically, now that I had Canadian citizenship, it was time was to move on. There was no point of staying in Ottawa without a full time job. I went to Massachusetts and wrote the NCLEX exam and I remember the computer shot off after the 75th question. That meant I had either done very well, or very poorly, and the computer had decided not to test me any longer. But I felt pretty good about the exam, and in three days the results came...I passed! One week later my Massachusetts Registered Nurse license came in the mail, and the next day I had a full-time job as an RN for the 11-7 shift at Buckley Nursing Home. It was my first professional licensed position in North America. Lucia also received her U.S Cosmetology license and found a part-time job at a salon.

From here on, life started to change for the better. Thank you, Lord,!

Chapter 29
Graduate School

Working the night shift at the Nursing Home was not an easy task. During the day and evening shifts there were more nurses on the floor, but on nights you are alone with two CNAs for 40 patients. The second part of the month was always busier because of the editing that needed to be done for the coming month. All the orders for each patient required checking; and writing additional orders that were not preprinted was a common practice.

I was making a decent salary compared to my previous jobs, and combined with Lucia's salary, this permitted us to buy a two-family house within ten months. My parents moved into one of the apartments, and this helped to make the mortgage payments on time, and even slip in an extra payment now and then. However, human nature is rarely satisfied with the status quo, and I was dreaming of an opportunity to advance beyond being a registered nurse.

Victoria also wanted to start ice skating lessons, but I thought piano classes would be better for her. We found a teacher in the neighborhood and took her there. She lasted only three classes. I could see, she didn't like it, Lucia was insisting that she continues in the hopes that Victoria would change her mind, however it is hard to judge what a six-year-old really likes. So, we gave it a try, but it didn't work. Today, Victoria is asking Lucia "Mom, why did you allow Dad to allow me to stop practicing piano? I could have been good if I continued!" Lucia tells her now it's never too late to learn! Okay, then we decided to take her to the ice rink. Lucia also dreamed about this when she was a young girl, but there were no ice rinks in Moldova, except for the frozen Prut River Valley in the winter. Shortly after, Victoria joined the Greenfield Area Figure Skating Club and started her skating career. She became a good solo skater and started competing in different skating competitions around Massachusetts. Every day after school she would go to the skating rink and practice for two hours. We remember her growing up with bruises around her body from falling so much during practice, but she loved it.

At the same time, Lucia was balancing Nicole's pageants where she competed in four different pageants across the United States in her childhood years. She won second place in her first National American Miss pageant that awarded her the opportunity to visit and compete in California at another pageant where she placed second in the Spokesmodel competition. Nicole loved meeting new people and speaking, performing, and showing her personality on stage. Lucia was also taking Nicole to guitar lessons every week, which she continues to play to this day.

Continuing my graduate school journey, I researched the schools in the proximity, and found a Nurse Anesthetist program in Hartford, CT. When I contacted them, they wanted me to come for twenty-seven months - five days a week. I asked if the curriculum could be accommodated for my needs, since I already had an anesthesiologist license in the past. They told me that education as an anesthesiologist was not equivalent to nurse anesthetist education. So, this option was removed from my list.

Then I went to Springfield College and met with the Physician's Assistant program director… same answer - two full years of study, five days per week. My work schedule would not allow for this. By this time, I had been hired to be the Clinical Nursing Supervisor for the 3-11 shift at Franklin Medical Center. I needed to work at least two week days, and all the weekends, to be able to continue to work in that capacity. The last option left on my list was the Nurse Practitioner

Program at the University of Massachusetts, Amherst. I went to the open house meeting and had a discussion with the faculty. I found out that this program would fit in my work schedule. But, in order to get into this program which was part of the Graduate School, I needed a bachelor's degree in nursing. I did not have that; only an associate degree from Algonquin College in Ottawa. I met with several faculty members, and I can't remember all the details of how this went, but at the end they told me that I could challenge some exams, and take just two undergraduate level courses in order to meet the bachelors in nursing requirement. So, I took a leadership in nursing 3.0 credit course, and community nursing, also a 3.0 credit course. After completing these courses and taking two exams I was admitted to grad school in the Family Nurse Practitioner Program.

I recall those years being the busiest time in my career. I had no free weekends for two years, but because my shifts were from 3-11p.m., Sunday morning was open to attend church and play guitar in the praise team. Looking back, I can see God's hand orchestrating my schedule.

Studying the medical disciplines in that program felt like a refresher to me, but the graduate nursing course was a nightmare. Nursing research, nursing theory, advance concepts of practice, etc. required lots of study time to write those papers. I really believe that it was God's plan for me to work as a clinical supervisor during those years. I remember running around the hospital with the clipboard, numerous trips between the pharmacy and ER, but at the same time having time to return to the office and spend time in front of the computer, studying and writing papers. During the summer and winter intersession I did the clinical practicum hours, and all it paid off. After two years I received a Master's Degree in Nursing and the Family Nurse Practitioner Certification.

I was one step closer to practicing medicine again.

Chapter 30
Department of State

One day while reading through a medical journal, I found an ad asking for Nurse Practitioners or Physician Assistants willing to work for the State Department as a Foreign Service Health Practitioner. It was required that every two years, those working in State Department postings abroad, be switched. To be considered for a job, you needed to hold a license in one of the States, and a DEA certification. Knowledge of a foreign language was a plus. The positions were at U.S. Embassies around the world, and the job description was to provide primary care for Embassy personnel. If a patient required further medical treatment, a medical evacuation plan was in place. It sounded like an interesting position; working for the federal government with all its' benefits. I applied, but received no contact for over six months. Then one day I got an email to come to Washington for an interview. What I didn't know, was that before they invited me for the interview, FBI and DOS agents had been in Greenfield interviewing my neighbors, and colleagues at my new work place in ER, as part of my security clearance.

In Washington they gave me forty-five minutes to write a composition paper on one of three or four topics provided. I remembered in grad school taking a leadership course and writing about the pros and cons of a Universal Health Care System for everyone in the U.S. versus Private Insurance/HMO/Medicare/Medicaid, so I wrote about that.

After finishing this paper, I had to wait for about a half an hour, and then I was called in for the interview. There were two physicians and a nurse practitioner who interviewed me. They asked questions on different clinical situations from emergency medicine to something as simple as cold symptoms. There were questions dealing with mental health as well. The interview took no longer than one hour, and then I was asked to wait until the committee made their decision. Because I was entering as a nurse practitioner, the director for the mid level providers came to inform me that I was offered the position as a Foreign Service Health Practitioner, or "FSHP". I thanked her for the offer, and left the office of medical services at the DOS to catch the evening flight back to Bradley.

In a few months an official letter came that delineated all the details about the training I needed to complete at the Foreign Service Institute in Arlington, VA. I was included in the 83rd Foreign Service Specialist Class, and started the training in March. In Washington DC springtime was at the door, and there was no snow, ice, or cold weather. The class material was so intense and compact that, in the evenings, I left the FSI with headaches. Very interesting stuff was presented to us. We had different speakers every day, including Ambassadors, DCMs, and other officials. Because I was fluent in two other languages, I decided to test so that I could get a raise in salary. The Romanian language wasn't on the list for a raise, but Russian was. There would be a ten percent increase in salary for those passing the test at level three minimum. I passed at a five for the spoken part and four for writing and comprehension. The maximum level was five.

We went to the CIA headquarters in Virginia for additional in-service and were amazed at the number of people in that building at any one point in time. I am not telling the actual number, but it is in the thousands. There is a small hospital/emergency room right there in that building. I saw advanced medical technology, allowing medical service operatives anywhere in the world to talk to, and video stream live, to a physician at headquarters. While there, I saw how a PA in the mountains of Nepal was getting further instructions on an injured agent. It was fascinating, but I didn't want to be in his shoes.

The swearing-in ceremony into the Diplomatic Corps was getting close, as was the training. We were told that the Secretary of State, Condoleezza Rice would be there to perform it. The day before the ceremony Lucia came to Washington to be present at the ceremony. She went with other family members present for special protocol instructions and additional security clearance before were allowed into the State Department building. The auditorium was nice and large. I think there were between forty and fifty Foreign Service Specialists being sworn in that day. There were only three of us from the medical service. A physician from Illinois was going to be the Regional Medical Officer in Lagos, Nigeria, a physician assistant going to U.S. Embassy in Liberia, Monrovia as a Foreign Service Health Practitioner, or FSHP, and I was a family nurse practitioner going to the U.S. Embassy in Moscow for three to four months, and then to Tashkent, Uzbekistan for two years as a FSHP. In Moscow, there were around three hundred Americans working at the embassy; but in Tashkent I would have only ninety people. The initial posting for me was at the Embassy in Abuja, Nigeria, but because they didn't have an English high school there for Victoria, I didn't take it. We had the opportunity to have Victoria in a private boarding school, and the State Department would pay for it, but we thought having her with us, where we could all see each other every day, was a better option.

Just before the beginning of the ceremony the head of the Foreign Service Institute announced that because of the pope's death, (John Paul II) President George Bush and Secretary of State Condoleezza Rice would be attending the burial in Rome, and she would not be there that morning. You could hear an audible "Ahhhh," a disappointed breath of everyone. All of us were looking forward to seeing and meeting the secretary. Instead, he said that the Undersecretary, Nicholas Burns, would be there.

When he arrived, we all had to rise, and repeat after him the pledge: "I,…... .so help me God." Then we had pictures taken with him and other officials. The festivity of that day raised our emotions and excitement. Lucia started dreaming of living in Moscow and her mother coming often to visit us, since it is only a two hour flight from

Moldova. Both girls would study at the English-American School in Moscow. In Tashkent they had an English high school as well.

A few days after the ceremony, all our family members received diplomatic passports. I was scheduled to go first, and Lucia and the girls would join me in June when the school year was over. Going to Moscow again…this was quite an experience. Our hopes and dreams about the journey lay before us, and we lived every day with anticipation.

Chapter 31
Residency training

There was just a little over a week left before my departure to the U.S. Embassy in Moscow, but for some reason, I didn't feel that I would make it there.

When the Canadian residency matching results were posted online, I logged into my profile, and to my surprise, I noticed that I matched into the Dalhousie Family Medicine Residency Program in Halifax, Nova Scotia. It was a bitter-sweet feeling. I had questions: "Why now? My career appeared to be settled. Why did I not match in previous years?" I tried to answer those questions, rationalizing why. For this match, I had applied for anesthesia and family medicine, but before I had applied only for anesthesia. Probably that was why I did not match in the last two years.

This was a very difficult time for me, trying to make the right decision. In a way, it was great news because for years this is what I had been waiting for. On the other hand, it seemed to me that the Foreign Service career was an opportunity to work for the federal government and to have diplomatic status wherever I went. To provide primary care to the ambassadors, DCMs and their families was a challenge; but also, prestigious. After struggling with this for a few days, I decided to ask the residency program director to postpone my enrollment for one year. I thought, if I worked overseas for a year, I would get a sense if that job was something I wanted to do long term.

But, she told me that if I didn't start the program on July 1st when all the residents began their PGY-1 year, I needed to resign. That meant I would have to reapply for matching again later on, with no guarantee that I would match again.

I went to the director of medical services at the DOS and explained my situation. He was very understanding and told me sincerely, "I wouldn't want to be in your shoes. This is a very difficult decision for you. In my experience here at the DOS, no one has resigned from this job once hired, but I'll respect whatever decision you make." I spoke with my dad on the phone about this, and he suggested that I leave Washington and go to Halifax to start the residency. He told me that this had been my goal for many years, and while the new job might appear prestigious and interesting, it would not give me the license to be a medical doctor again. I had been waiting for this moment for many years, and now that I was accepted, why was I was having second thoughts? That night I couldn't sleep. Conflicting thoughts about working in Moscow at the embassy, or being a family medicine resident would not let me fall asleep. I had been praying that God would show me a sign, or give me peace in the choice I had to make. Somehow, I snoozed for a while, and then the phone rang and woke me up. It was Lucia calling. She could not sleep either, and had been praying over this as well. While she really wanted us to start this new career, and she preferred that we go to Moscow, she also knew my dream and desire to get the medical license. "Come home," is the only thing she told me.

I needed to hear that. Now I had confirmation from two people who were close to me. There was no more "sitting on the fence" feeling. I sent an email to medical services with a resignation letter attached. I took my stuff, and in seven hours I was home.

A few weeks later we drove to Halifax with two cars. It was a twelve hour trip, but it didn't feel long. The first day there, Lucia and the girls enjoyed the harbor, the scenery and the shopping, while I went for an all day in-service. The second day we had an information session at the department of family medicine where I got a pager, the rotation schedule, a call schedule, and met my faculty advisor, etc. Later that day I got a name tag with inscriptions "M.D., Family Medicine Resident." For a moment I felt like a fresh graduate just starting residency. However, for me this was the second time. Even more, I was the second oldest resident in the whole Dalhousie Family Medicine Residency Program of over 40 people!

Once we got on the wards, the attending physicians could see each one of us more closely. I can surely say that all my previous experience as a physician and later on as a registered nurse and nurse practitioner helped me feel more confident and capable of doing much more than an average PGY-1. I remember very well the ER rotation at QE II, where I had many opportunities to practice the acute care skills. At the end of the PGY-1 year everyone got two months of electives. Guess what I chose? Yes, anesthesia. I had not done any anesthesia for eight years by that time, and had to re-learn how to ride the bicycle again. Slowly it all came back; with the difference being that now I had an advanced anesthetic machine with all the bells and whistles, which I did not have when I trained and worked in Moldova. Back there, I remembered sharing a portable O2 saturation monitor between three or four operating rooms. A manual BP cuff, a stethoscope, the patient's skin and mucous membranes were the only monitors in those days.

During the PGY-2 year we had to do a three-month rural rotation and I chose Woodstock, New Brunswick. Initially, I didn't know anything about Dr. McLaughlin who was the preceptor there affiliated with our residency program. My choice was based solely on convenience - Woodstock was the closest town to the U.S. border. From there to my home in Massachusetts was only little over 400 miles, compared to close to 800 miles from Halifax. But, when I arrived there and started working with Dr. McLaughlin, my choice happened to be the right one from all the aspects. He was a great teacher, extremely experienced, a walking encyclopedia. He had a busy office, and also was doing ER call, inpatient work and obstetrics. I don't think there are many doctors left who do all of the above. I enjoyed working there, and have a great respect and appreciation for him… a truly rural physician who inspired me to consider working in a rural hospital after completing residency.

Chapter 32
Anesthesia training

Time flies fast when you're having fun, and my residency program in family medicine was coming to an end. During my rural rotation with Dr. McLaughlin, the medical recruiter from the New Brunswick Region 3 Health Authority offered me a position at the new Upper River Valley Hospital that was scheduled to open in 2007. I already had an interest in rural medicine, and this had only solidified at the completion of my rural rotation, largely due to the influence of my preceptor. I knew that if I joined them, I could work as a family, or an ER physician. However, my greatest desire for all these years had been to be able to practice anesthesia again. I had tried to get into anesthesia in the past, but didn't match. Now after finishing family residency, I had an opportunity to go for one extra year in anesthesia and obtain a license as a GP-Anesthetist. This was the fastest way to get into anesthesia practice. The other choice was to complete a Royal College anesthesia program, but that required four more years of residency. Considering the timing, and my age, I decided to go for GP-Anesthesia.

When I started searching for programs, I found out that most of them were in Ontario, or Western Canada. The closest program to Massachusetts was at Queens University in Kingston, Ontario. I had promised my family that there would be no more training after I finished family medicine. I couldn't even imagine what Lucia would say when she hears that I wanted to do an extra year of residency. By then she had been living alone with the girls for almost three years. I was only the monthly visitor, and was missing how much the girls were growing and changing during that time. One day when Lucia's sister was there visiting, I told her my plans. You should have seen my wife's facial expression! Denial…unbelief…upset... probably all of the above. It took some work between me and her sister for her to accept the fact that I was not moving home for at least another year; but to move everyone else to be with me wasn't a good idea either. Lucia had been working for the Greenfield Public School for seven years by then, and Victoria and Nicole had their routines between school, ice skating and music lessons. It would be too much of a change for them to accommodate me. We decided to leave things the way they were.

After applying for the position at Queens I found out that because I was a foreign graduate, I wasn't eligible for a postgraduate training position in Ontario, even though I already had a full license as a family physician in Canada. In order to receive funding from the Ministry of Health of Ontario, I needed to finish family medicine residency in Ontario. I had completed it in Halifax, Nova Scotia. This was just another stumbling block in my way. But by that time I had learned how to overcome difficulties, so this wasn't anything new to me. However, I needed to start the training. There must be a way to do it and I kept asking myself "how?" over and over. I had been praying about it, and felt peace that this was going to work out. I asked the GP-Anesthesia Program Director from Queens about getting the funding from a different province, and he said that he would look into it. A few days later I got an email stating that if another province paid the university for my training, I could start the anesthesia in July with the rest of the residents. Here was where the recruiter from New Brunswick was going to come in handy. I asked the Region 3 Health Authority to pay for my training in exchange for a "return of service" contract. The agreement was one year of return of service work for each year of training.

Wow! What would Lucia say? Now I'd be gone for at least two more years. I prayed "O God, please help me." I wanted to do it; I needed to do it. This time Lucia wasn't as surprised as before.

She understood very well what was ahead of us. During that year I was able to come home more often, as Kingston was only a little over five hours from Massachusetts.

The training went fast, and there I was a year later, with a certificate to practice GP-Anesthesia in my hands. I had finally arrived! My dream had come true! I thought I deserved a pat on the back. I realized though, that it was only because of God's grace. The words of Apostle Paul came to mind: "I can't consider myself a winner yet and count not myself to have apprehended. One thing that I need to do now is to forget the things that are behind and press toward the things that are before."

I can't live with my yesterday's accomplishments and experiences. I only can learn from them; but I need to live in the present and look to the future.

The new hospital had just opened and the position was waiting for me there. When I came to the Upper River Valley Hospital I fell in love with it immediately. It was a brand-new facility with gorgeous, fully integrated operating rooms, state of the art equipment, etc. I joined the other three anesthetists there, and we became a well-functioning department that provided 24 hours a day, 365 days a year anesthetic coverage for the hospital.

That one year return of service also passed very quickly, and my commitment was fulfilled. Nothing else would preclude me from leaving the hospital. So, I moved back to Massachusetts with my family, and started to work in the ER. I could not practice anesthesia in the U.S. because of different training I had in Canada.

But I couldn't leave the URVH completely. I find myself, even two years later, still driving up there every month for a seven or eight day rotation, providing anesthesia service for that community. It has become dear to me, very special. In the last two years I've had three different anesthesia positions offered to me in Ontario, but I haven't accepted them. I don't think it is a guilty feeling in leaving URVH, because they were the ones who sent me for training and gave me the position in the first place. It is more than that. It's because I have nice colleagues to work with, and friendly people in the community, and have found some special friends there, Dale and Judy. Whenever I work there each month, I visit with them and feel like they are my second family. I thank God for them.

So now, three weeks out of the month I am an ER physician in Massachusetts, and one week per month I am the anesthesiologist on call at URVH in New Brunswick, Canada. I've got the best of both worlds. How long this is going to last, God only knows.

Upper River Valley Hospital; Waterville, NB, Canada

Epilogue

Year after year were passing fast. After 10 long Canadian winters my Raynaud's phenomenon got to a point that I had to move to a warmer climate. This played in handy for Lucia as she has been whispering in my ear for many years to move south, Charlotte area being her preference. It was hard to accept the fact that I'll not be able to practice anesthesia, but as Ecclesiastes said "To everything there is a season, a time for every purpose under heaven. He has made everything beautiful in its time. Also, He has put eternity in their hearts. I know that nothing is better for them to rejoice, and to do good in their lives, and also that every man should eat and drink and enjoy the good of his labor – it is the gift of God"

Yes, I can testify to it. He has been very good to us. Blessed us beyond our expectation. So, my reader, if I have to tell you just one thing, here it is: Don't give up. In this country you can achieve anything you desire if you work hard!

I enjoy very much working in the ER at Providence Heath - Fairfield, a faith based and mission driven organization. Lucia continues her career as a cosmetologist and also continues to provide her tutor and interpreter services to the Greenfield Public Schools District. Victoria has finished medical school and awaiting the residency match. Nicole graduated from university and was accepted into law school. We don't know what tomorrow holds, but I know Who holds tomorrow. One thing that I do know for sure is that we must remain faithful to Him, and He will never leave us nor forsake us. That's a promise.

Victoria, Lucia, Sergei and Nicole Ivantchev - 2020